LOVE, LOSS,
and
DEMENTIA

Stories About Our Parents with Dementia

and a Validation of Your Journey

by Lauren Austin

and Holly Gershbein

"Current estimates indicate 35.6 million people worldwide are living with dementia... This number will double by 2030 and more than triple by 2050."

"Dementia doesn't just affect individuals. It also affects and changes the lives of family members."

-World Health Organization

WHO Library Cataloguing-in-Publication Data: Dementia: a public health priority. 1. Aging – psychology. 2.Dementia – epidemiology. 3.Dementia – prevention and control. 4. Caregivers – psychology. 5. Health services for the aged – economics. 6. Long-term care. 7. Health priorities. I. World Health Organization. ISBN 978 92 4 156445 8 (NLM classification: WM 200) © World Health Organization 2012

Praise for Love, Loss and Dementia

"*Love, Loss and Dementia* is truly inspiring. It touches on every aspect of what it is to have a loved one with this dreadful disease...very insightful and touches the heart of the reader. Truly brilliant!"
  -Jackie G.

"I loved it!!! It was very relevant and very inspirational...I congratulate you on your dedication to help others in this very challenging chapter of life on earth. It is a 'dark chapter' indeed, but every chapter has a beginning and an end.... Your wisdom...will help others to know they are not alone...Caregiving is about thriving, not just surviving this journey."
  -Peggy Ann R.

"I felt the emotions in *Love, Loss and Dementia* and almost felt like I knew the authors' mothers personally. It is very hard to lose a loved one and many times, I felt the authors knew how I felt when I lost my dad. We are not alone."
  -Nava I.

"It took me four readings of *Love, Loss and Dementia* to get through it without tears blurring the words. How I wish it had been available when we were going through our own mother's illnesses. The circumstances of dementia invading my family's world were similar and painful, and, sadly, the results were the same... There is precious little available for families who face the disease. The support group that I attended a couple of times was ok, not very well run, and had no professional help to explain to us what to expect. Your book took care of all of that and should be there for families, whether they are participating in the care of the relative or not.
  -Pat P.

After reading *Love, Loss and Dementia*, I like the way it makes you feel at ease. It would have been nice to have a book like this when I needed it to show me how other people dealt with these issues.

-***Randy N.***

Table of Contents

Foreword

This book provides guidance, comfort, perspective and resources. More than that, *Love, Loss and Dementia* is a narrative of determination and advocacy. It portrays the inexorable cognitive decline of a loved one, and its impact on family and friends. It lifts the shade on a private window, allowing us to perceive an array of the authors' emotions. We glimpse their struggle, while still providing care and support.

Although this book is written to assist caregivers and family, it serves much more. It addresses making difficult decisions that have no good options, acceptance of the inevitable, and the isolation of the caregiver. It screams advocacy, and suggests non-conventional solutions. It also legitimizes and validates those emotions experienced by all those close to the patient. This book is also a vehicle for healing, for both the authors and readers, bringing some closure to their painful journey.

I read this book from a unique perspective; that of a brother to one of the authors, a friend to the other, as well as a son and a neurologist. I now better appreciate my sister's frustration and her covenant with my mother. She never gave up or vacillated in her efforts to improve my mother's quality of life. As a son and a neurologist, I was my mother's medical advocate, but never her physician. Mom was always my mother, never my patient. As physicians do, I tried to be objective. And medical decisions were not made by me alone, but by family consensus. I think, in retrospect, my objectivity served as a defense and as an emotional cushion.

I tell medical students that as dementia progresses, my attention shifts to the wellbeing of the caregiver. They face a lack of recognition, inconsistent support, inadequate public and financial resources, and oftentimes burnout. The authors' depictions of their experiences are authentic, and will assist all who read this book in becoming a more informed partner in the care team.

Dr. Elliott Schulman
Philadelphia, Pennsylvania

Section One

Beginnings

Why Am I Reading This Book?

Do you have a loved one with dementia?

Have you ever felt at a loss as to what to do about an aging relative who can no longer take care of themselves?

Are you unable to care for your loved one at home because of finances or other reasons?

Are your family members arguing about your loved one's care plan?

Do you have a loved one who is about to go into a nursing home or is already in a nursing home?

Are you a long-distance caregiver?

Are you an advocate for someone who cannot advocate for themselves?

Are you at odds with the advice of professionals with respect to your loved one's care?

Would you feel supported knowing that others share your feelings and can validate what's happening in your life?

If your answer is "yes" to any of the above questions, then our book, which touches on these issues, will provide you with support and guidance. Each chapter will take you on a very introspective and heartfelt journey into our lives, with the hope that you will find comfort in knowing that you are not alone as you travel down similar roads.

Introduction

Holly

To Our Readers...

This book was written as a labor of love, and it is dedicated in honor of our mothers, Rose and Bertha.

Lauren and I have been lifelong friends. Our parents were also friends. We went through grammar school, high school and college together. Although Lauren and I currently live in two different cities many miles apart, we still maintain a close bond and communicate daily. Rose is Lauren's mom and Bertha is my mom, and I speak of them in the present tense because they are always with us.

Lauren and I shared the experience of our moms having dementia and ultimately being placed in a nursing home. In fact, unbeknownst to each other, when we were young, we had both promised ourselves and our parents that we would never allow them to go into a nursing home when they got older. But both moms became ill, and we were each left with no other viable choice. Safety and finances made the decision for both of us.

It is so important to be able to talk to someone who truly understands what you are feeling when a loved one has dementia and/or has to go into a nursing home. Many times, people don't know how to react or what to say. I looked to the professionals to soothe my emotional pain, but in retrospect, perhaps they couldn't respond in any meaningful way because what I was experiencing was not something that they had personally gone through.

We wrote this book with the expectation that our experiences would be helpful for others who are either going through, or will be going through the same or similar path. We wanted you to know that no matter how you might be feeling, you are not alone. Lauren and I hope that you find comfort and encouragement in reading about our respective journeys, and how we faced every challenge along the way.

About the Author

Holly

My family means the world to me. My parents gave us life and love. Growing up in Buffalo, New York, I have wonderful memories of times spent with family and close friends. I keep those images close to my heart and wouldn't trade them for anything. My mom and dad were wonderful parents.

My parents were Bertha (Bert) and Morris (Morry or Moishe), and my older brother's name is Alan. Alan and I were the center of their universe. My parents weren't strict, but very supportive and loving, and steered us in the right direction, obviously telling us when we were off course. Both parents worked, but mom actually stayed home until we were in high school. My maternal grandmother, born in Kiev, lived with us and spoke broken English. However, I understood her when she was upset with me. I loved her dearly and was devastated when she passed away. Actually, it was the day of a massive blizzard and the doctor was unable to come over to check on her. We lived in a double story house, with my aunt, uncle and cousins directly upstairs. That is probably why I love to be around family, and would not want to live alone.

My mom had a beautiful and caring aura about her. She placed her family above everything else. She was the caregiver of us all. The youngest of four sisters and one brother, mom was the central force behind our entire family. Everyone knew her as "Bert" or "Bertha" or "Mrs. G" or "Gramma" but I knew her as "mom". Every event and holiday gathering was hosted by my mom at our house. My friends loved to come over because my mom would bake cookies, play cards and welcomed them with open arms. She always had an occasion to celebrate and opened her home to anyone who knocked on the door. I loved it when people told me, "You're just like your mom." I consider that to be the highest compliment that anyone could give me. In her later years, we talked to each other at least three times a day. I lived in Houston and she lived in Buffalo. Each day I'd call to make sure she was ok and ask about her day, and at night I called to say, "Good night - I love you." I miss her words "Hi doll" or "I love you". While I know that all mother-daughter relationships are not like ours, I wanted to give you an idea as to how my mother and I operated together, and how close we were. After her communication started to deteriorate because of her dementia, she still attempted to say those words. Some things eradicated by illness can still be held fast by love. My mom and Lauren's mom were lifelong friends, and they brought the two of us together in kindergarten.

My dad was a practical jokester and loved to make toys for us as he was extremely handy. He was a gentle soul and a fabulous dad. He always had time to take us on outings to the beach, to the zoo, or anywhere for that matter, and he was an excellent cook. I could always depend on him to help me whenever I needed a replacement car, or to pick up my friends and bring them over, or even just to hang out together and laugh. He was born in Chicago, and had two brothers who ultimately resided in California. My dad had polio as a young boy, but he rarely complained and always had a smile on his face.

Later in life, he had post-polio syndrome, which, along with his strokes, disabled him. The doctor said that my mom wouldn't survive if we didn't institute round-the-clock care for him. Since this wasn't financially possible, we worked with a geriatric care manager, and placed him in the closest and best facility. My mom and my brother visited my dad every day, and I would come to visit every few months from my home in Houston. I could no longer converse with my dad through daily phone calls once he lost his ability to speak. My line to him was through my brother and my mom. It was devastating because I never thought either of my parents would go to a nursing facility. Also, as a speech pathologist, it was devastating that I could no longer communicate with dad on a daily basis with words.

In the Introduction to this book, I told you that Lauren and I wrote the book in honor of our mothers, but it also honors our fathers because we were both fortunate in that we each had wonderful dads. For me, the pain of having both parents end up in a nursing home, albeit at different times, was unbearable, and to this day leaves a scar on my heart. I will say that my family, as well as some of my cousins, helped in many ways in which they may not be aware. I know that without my husband, my family, my children and friends, I wouldn't have been able to cope...and I thank them for that.

At present, I currently reside in Richmond, Texas with my loving and supportive husband, Henry Rothschild and my dogs Gumbo and Fay. My educational background consists of a B.S. in Social Work and an M.S. in Communication Disorders.

About the Author

Lauren

I grew up in Buffalo, New York, the younger of two children. My parents were Morris ("Morry" or "Moe") and Rose ("Rosie" or "Cute Girl"), and my older brother's name is Elliott. Education was always a priority in my family, and my brother and I knew that college was mandatory for us. My parents, both bright, were never given the opportunity to go to college and they wanted a better life for their children. My father, the oldest of four, lost his mother at age 16, and was forced to go to work right out of high school so that he could help to provide for his younger siblings. My mother, the second youngest, and the only girl out of four children, also went to work after high school because her father wanted her to help pay for her brothers' college education.

My parents followed what was then the traditional path. My dad worked and my mother stayed home taking care of us. We were close to our relatives on both sides of the family and visited them on weekends. Sometimes we would go to visit older relatives who lived in a nursing home. I HATED that place; it was always so depressing because no one ever seemed to talk or smile. Every time we went there, I would promise my parents that I would always take care of them, and they would never have to go into a nursing home.

I had a very good childhood. I never wanted for anything, and there were generally lots of laughs and practical joking going on. My dad's only real vice was smoking cigars, and my brother would randomly load his cigars with something to make them explode. The explosion always happened to my dad at the most inopportune times – I remember it once happening at a wedding - but he never got angry; he just laughingly bellowed "YOU KIDS!" He loved a good joke, and had a new one ready to tell you all the time. My dad was fairly easy-going on most things, though very stubborn on certain issues, and never at a loss for words. He was so well-liked at his independent living community that he became known as its "honorary mayor". He loved his family, and whenever we visited my parents at their independent living apartment, my dad always proudly introduced us to all the new residents.

My mother was definitely the stricter parent; the one who wielded the orange belt across our behinds when we did not behave. Due to my father's work schedule, my mother was also the parent who came to our plays and recitals, and helped us with our schoolwork. When I was upset, she was the one who always told me "things will be better tomorrow."

My mother was also our staunchest advocate. If she felt that we were not being treated fairly by a teacher at school, or anyone for that matter, she would immediately speak to the "wrongdoer" and defend us to the bitter end. She was a lioness, and my brother and I were her cubs.

My mom was never one to mince words in any situation. She told it like she saw it, whether you liked it or not. Conversely, she was also very sensitive, and when her feelings got hurt, she held on to the hurt for a long time. She could be very funny, and had a great laugh. She supported us through thick and thin, and could always be counted on for advice and a sympathetic ear.

Her mother (my grandmother) lived with us until I was about five, when she passed away. My mother was very close to her mother, and so was I. My grandmother was very kind and loving. There is one memory that really stands out for me - that of a blind boy around my age who lived one street away from us. Since my active imagination convinced me that I was going to wake up blind one day, I would practice walking around the neighborhood hanging on to my grandmother's arm with my eyes closed, and feeling around to take my next steps by using her cane. Neither my mother nor my father would indulge me in this undertaking, but my grandmother walked me up and down nearby streets for as long as I wanted, for days on end. I remember her with so much love, and I am sure that she was the catalyst for the special empathy that I feel for seniors.

As I graduated from college, moved away, married and started a family, my parents were right there, sharing every new experience with me. How I wish that things could have stayed the way they were! However, as my mother's arthritis worsened over the years, it started affecting other parts of her body. My brother, a neurologist (who runs a well-known headache clinic for migraine sufferers), managed her medical care, and despite his excellent oversite, her mobility became more and more compromised. I actively began researching as to how I could best help her, and subsequently utilized all types of resources and support to enable her to remain at home as long as possible. However, ultimately, we, as a family, realized that a move was essential, and the rest of the story can be found in the ensuing sections of this book.

My love for my family and passion for helping others led me to pursue my Master's in Social Work. Several years later, I graduated from law school in California, and worked for more than a decade as an attorney. After taking time off to care for my children, I returned to my social work roots, focusing on facilitating international adoptions. Since 2011, I have been working as a Senior Care Manager, which I now realize had been one of the roles that I had taken on with respect to my mother's care. My goal is to be a staunch advocate for my clients, and help them to remain independent for as long as possible within the context of their safety, finances and the availability of community resources.

I currently reside in Jacksonville, Florida with Dana, my husband of over thirty years, and my 18-year-old daughter, Jessica. Fortunately for me, my son Daniel and his partner Ron, who recently got married, also live in Jacksonville and we all get together frequently. Family is and will always be my number one priority, just as it was for my parents.

Find Your Smile

Holly

As my mom's dementia progressed, a friend said to me "Go Find Your Smile." I took it to mean that I should seek out things that would make me happy. At the time, depression set in and I never thought that I would feel happiness for myself, as my focus was on trying to do everything that I could think of to make my mom happy and to help her find her smile. As her condition worsened, all the things that had always brought her pleasure, such as reading, crosswords, playing Canasta, entertaining and being with friends, were no longer of interest to her. It has been several years since mom's passing and I still miss her terribly, although my good days far outnumber the bad ones. I am able to smile much more because instead of focusing solely on her loss, I can now recognize how fortunate I was to have had her for my mom. She was a remarkable woman who raised me to be kind, compassionate and tenacious. There is so much of her that I carry with me...her gestures, her voice, her mannerisms, and yes, her smile.

Lauren and I feel certain that our mission is to bring hope, inspiration, and understanding to others who are traveling down the same roads that we traveled with our mothers. These are our personal stories, warts and all. No one is prepared for this life change, no matter how strongly you may believe that you are. It is a physical, mental, and emotional endurance race that will test you to the limits. Be aware that if you choose to be an active participant in the life of your loved one who is facing the challenges of dementia, you should be prepared for a very bumpy ride. Whether you are single or married, whether you have very young children, or even adult children, you will discover guidelines within this book to help you more successfully navigate dementia care, the nursing home experience, or even disagreements with family about care planning.

We hope that this book will not only help those who are caregiving for a parent, but also those who are caregivers for spouses, children, relatives, neighbors or friends. If you know anyone who is a caregiver, be a friend and give them a copy of the book. It is essential for caregivers to know that they are not alone, and there are other people who have gone through the same journey before them. Future caregivers will also have a much better understanding of possible situations that may eventually affect their lives. This book will provide them with suggestions and recommendations as to how to cope, but most importantly, it will validate their feelings. They will be grateful that you thought of them as this book addresses issues that may be close to their hearts. You may want to write a short note on the inside cover saying that you were thinking of them. I would venture to say that they will find **their** smile because you helped them in ways you cannot imagine. There is no road map or tutorial for this journey, but perhaps our insights will prevent you, or someone you know, from making a few of the same mistakes that we made, or will shed light on some of the joys that you can create along the way.

Section Two

Difficult Decisions

Transitioning and Downsizing

Lauren

After one of my mother's numerous hospitalizations, followed by a stint in a rehabilitation unit, she was ready to be released. The doctors advised us not to bring her home because she was experiencing more and more difficulty walking with her walker, and her home was not handicap accessible. They suggested that she remain on the "campus" where she had just had treatment, and consider moving into an independent living apartment or the assisted living facility. (In addition to the rehab unit, the campus housed an independent living facility, an assisted living facility, and a nursing home unit).

Added to my mother's mobility issues, her arthritis was taking its toll, she seemed to be experiencing the very early stages of dementia, and most importantly, my dad could no longer adequately or safely take care of her. The family was faced with several choices to consider: (1) undertake renovations to my parents' home to make it handicap accessible and hire aides for my mother; (2) move both my mother and my father into an independent living apartment in a facility that had on-site home health providers, meals, activities and handicap accessibility; or, the least desirable choice; (3) split up my mom and dad into two different living situations, that is, my dad would stay in their home, and my mom would move into assisted living.

The agreement that the family finally reached was that my father, who had less than zero desire to move, would give the independent living facility a trial run for six months, and move from the home that my parents had owned since my brother and I were small. He was very hesitant about the idea, but agreed to do it for my mother's sake. The deal was that their home would remain empty for the length of the trial run period. If my father ended up not liking independent living, he would return home, and we explore all available options for my mother. If he did like the facility, my parents would retain ownership of their home, but we would try to find someone to rent it.

When my parents moved into independent living for that trial period, I packed for their transition by myself. (I hired professional movers for the actual move). My goal was to pack all their clothing and personal belongings, along with the minimum amount of furniture that they would need to get by on in their new two-bedroom apartment, leaving the remainder of the furniture in place in their own home. At this point in time, my family (my husband and one child at the time) and I were living in Florida. My brother and his family lived in Pennsylvania, and my parents lived in Buffalo, New York. I flew in to do the moving job myself. Although I grew up in Buffalo and still had good friends there, along with some aunts, uncles and cousins in the area, I really didn't want to impose on anyone, and actually didn't think that it would be too difficult for me to accomplish this "small" move on my own. How wrong I was!

It wasn't the physical aspect of packing, but rather the emotional aspect of having to go through drawers and boxes in order to pack what my parents needed that knocked me for a loop. Here I was going through years and years of belongings, reading early letters that my parents had written to each other before their marriage, and seeing reams of pictures of the family and extended family in much happier times. For the first time I came to the realization that my parents were entering into the final phase of their lives... that nothing would ever be the same... that the kinds of things that I was now doing for them, such as making decisions on their behalf, were the same kinds of things that I had always depended upon them to do for me. I didn't want it to be this way. I didn't want them to move out of the home that I had grown up in. I didn't want any part of this, and would have loved nothing better than to lock the door and magically fly back in time, when everything would be as I always remembered it to be whenever I came to visit. Unfortunately, time does march on... with or without your wanting it to. I cried and cried that day, sobbing so hard that when I spoke to my brother, he urged me to go to a local doctor to see if I could get a prescription for some tranquilizers to carry me through the move. I finished what I needed to do over the course of several days, and it was an extremely emotional time for me. One chapter was closing and another was opening, and I was deeply afraid that it would take me places that I did not want to go.

Ultimately, I came to understand that "change" does not mean necessarily mean "bad." Closing one chapter and opening another can be a good thing! I caused myself a lot of heartache when I anticipated the worst. If this is your situation, change your mindset and expect the best! My mom and dad turned out to be so happy during their initial years in their independent living apartment. My mom was getting the care that she needed, and best of all, my father was not responsible for giving it to her. They ate their evening meals in a lovely restaurant-type dining room every night, had social outlets, attended various activities, made some new friends, and re-connected with some old friends, all without having to go outside into the Buffalo winter weather. My father turned out to be extremely happy with the move, as he really blossomed socially, always took "newbies" under his wing, and never looked back! He became known as the "mayor" of their facility because he was so friendly and seemed to know everyone.

Due to the conditional nature of my parents' move to independent living, we were faced with several stages in their moving process. At the end of my father's trial period in the independent living facility, he happily agreed to continue living in independent living. At this point, we then moved their belongings from their home into storage so that the house could be rented. Down the road a few years, when the house was put up for sale, we had to clean out the basement and the attic, and we hauled those things that we wanted to keep, or were not sure about, to a large storage unit. Even though my brother and I and our families were involved in these subsequent moves, it still proved to be emotionally difficult for everyone.

As we moved furniture and other items into the large storage unit, my brother and I amicably decided what we each wanted for ourselves. Every time Elliott came to Buffalo, he stopped at the storage unit and removed more and more of his "keep" items to transport to his home. Although I kept downsizing the storage unit as it continued to empty, I never removed any of the things that I wanted to keep, even after both of my parents had passed away. I ultimately ended up paying for storage for far too long. Without question, my reluctance to clean out the unit and remove the last of my parents' possessions was governed by my emotional inability to fully accept their loss.

What I Learned:

- Talk with your mom and/or dad before there is even a move on the horizon, and ask them what they want to do with their personal keepsakes and old family pictures and albums. Suggest that they go through everything on their own, or even with your help, so that you aren't ultimately responsible for deciding what is important to them and what is not.

- If your parent(s) cannot guide you on downsizing, I recommend that you do not do this by yourself. Engage a sibling or close relative who can reminisce with you as you come upon things that jog family memories, and can also tell you that it is time to move on when you linger too long!

- If it is clear that something is not worth saving, don't save it! Throw away those chipped plates belonging to your grandmother, old magazines with interesting articles, etc. Arrange to have a trash company put a dumpster in place in the driveway for throwaways (as I did). The dumpster will be picked up and hauled away when you are ready for it to go. Otherwise, engage a service that will come to pick up all your trash on a designated day. (With my parents' first conditional move, I did not have to worry about what to do with furniture that was not being moved; it merely remained in the home).

- Understand the dimensions of the place being moved into, so as to make sure that what you plan to move will be able to fit into the new space.

- Make sure that you bring the things that you know are important to your loved ones...maybe it is that special table from your grandmother, or all the framed pictures. A "new" home that feels comfortable and familiar to your loved ones will help with their transition.

- If time is a factor for you, there are services that specialize in downsizing that will do all the packing up, as well as all the setting up at the other end. Some of these same services will even conduct estate sales to try to sell any leftover items of value.

- If your family members have antiques or other valuable items that will not be going with them, check with them to see if these items can be sold after an appraisal, or perhaps forwarded on early to the person or persons designated to inherit the items.

- I would discourage the storage of any items. If you find yourself in the unfortunate position of having to go through your loved ones' furnishings, belongings, etc., make your final disposition of items during your first go-round! Don't put items into a second pile (i.e. storage) in order to avoid figuring out what to do with them. If you don't want an item, but hate to throw it away because it has use, call Goodwill or the Salvation

Army and donate it to someone in need! If you want something, but it is too bulky to carry or ship, hire a moving company to pick it up and transport it to you. Guess what? In the end, I wound up throwing away many of my "keep" items and called Goodwill to pick up the rest! I could have saved myself years of storage fees if I had never stored anything to begin with!!

Tap into the Strengths of Family Members

Lauren

When it becomes clear that your loved one can no longer be cared for at home because they require a higher level of care and/or more hours of care than they are currently receiving, and there are no funds to hire this specialized or extra help, family members often come together in order to determine the next plan of action. Sometimes a nursing home turns out to be the only viable option. Despite the truth of this statement, making the decision to place your loved one in a nursing home may be agonizing to accept, and excruciatingly painful to put into place, as it certainly was for me.

For the nursing home resident, adjusting to their new environment can also be extremely difficult. In fact, the sad truth is that your relative may never adjust to it. I know that there were times that were better than others for my mother, but she never, not once, stopped wanting to go home. Let's face it, most nursing home environments do not replicate, or even come close to a comfortable home environment. I will tell you one thing, and I know that it was right for my situation…. I always tried to give my mother hope… I never said, and I would never allow anyone else to say in front of her, that she was never going to be able to go home. I always told her that she needed to work on getting better and getting stronger, and that we could talk to the doctor about coming home when she showed improvement.

When a close relative enters a nursing home, family dynamics will come into play because there is a change in the family structure. Families should be aware of trouble spots. Recognize that some family members may have a very difficult time accepting the nursing home reality, while others may not. While it is true that I have seen some situations where the transition is readily accepted, and family members divide up responsibilities easily, such as who is going to deal with the doctors, who is going to handle insurance, etc., this does not seem to be the norm. The situation that seems to occur most frequently is that one person in the family steps up to be the "primary", in other words, the person who takes on most of the responsibility for all facets of care for the nursing home resident, while others either take on a subordinate role or no role at all. (It is important to note that the "primary" may not necessarily want to be the primary, but is forced into that position because other relatives or siblings cannot or will not step up). Usually, the primary is the person who lives in the same city as the nursing home resident, but not always.

In one instance that I know of, an acquaintance who lived out-of-town acted as the primary for her father when he was moved to a nursing home, even though she had two sisters who each lived within 30 minutes of the nursing home. While the in-town sisters visited their dad on a regular basis, they were fairly complacent about his care, and always seemed OK with marginally acceptable standards. In other words, if their dad was not in any danger, they were alright with the minimum level of care that he received. The out-of-town sister wanted much more for her dad, and stayed on top of the nursing home staff on a daily basis to ensure that he received his Boost nutritional drink, that he was offered foods that he could chew, and that he was allowed to sleep in late, as was his habit.

Another major point of contention within the family can be financial. I am aware of situations where some siblings take the approach that any money spent on their mother or father in a nursing home is viewed as money taken directly out of their future inheritance. Therefore, they want any "extras" kept to the minimum, while other siblings are willing to spend any amount of money in order to bring comfort to the nursing home resident. If your relative in the nursing home is no longer competent to handle their own finances, hopefully, when they were competent, he or she had already prepared all the necessary documentation to appoint a Power of Attorney over their finances (usually a family member or close friend is picked to be Power of Attorney, although it can also be a professional, such as an attorney or accountant). If so, it would be the designated Power of Attorney who makes the ultimate decision over what is spent from the resident's assets for the resident's care. If there are no extra funds available, sometimes family members chip in to cover costs for the resident to use for extras. If some family members cannot or will not contribute, problems can ensue.

Some families completely fall apart after a parent goes into a nursing home; disagreements arise as to what could or should have been done to better help the parent before/after their admission into skilled nursing. If it is the mother who goes into a nursing home, and she is the one who held the siblings and extended family together, and also hosted all the family get-togethers, then these important family times may cease if no one else within the family can or will step in to take over.

Suffice it to say, whenever a parent or parents transition to a different stage in their lives, it results in a change in family dynamics, and relationships and responsibilities can become altered. This change happens even if family members live many miles apart from each other. You cannot change what is, but you can change how you accept the new "normal", and most importantly, how capably you deal with it.

What I Learned:

Feelings of anger and resentment don't have to tear families apart during this very difficult and stressful time. A very important concept to remember is that everyone views things from their own personal perspective. That is why, ultimately, even though *you* may be certain that you know what is best for your parent, your siblings may think that you have it all wrong and they have all the answers. You must understand that just because your relatives do not share *your* view, it doesn't mean that they are wrong and you are right, or vice versa. It simply means that their own life experiences have led them to a different conclusion.

If agreement over any issue, be it financial, medical, etc., cannot be readily achieved, talk it through and attempt to come to a compromise. As difficult as things may be with respect to having a parent who is a resident in a nursing home, problems will be compounded exponentially with the addition of siblings who are feuding. If necessary, consult with a Senior Care Manager to provide the family with an objective point of view for help in determining the best course of action for your relative.

A good way to work together is to sit down and discuss the tasks that need to be done in order to make sure that the nursing home resident receives the best possible care from every perspective. Tap into each person's strengths, and give them the tasks that they are best suited for, both from a professional and emotional standpoint. Try not to have any hidden agendas, and forget sibling rivalries and past resentments toward family members. Instead, come together and strictly focus as to what is in the best interests of the nursing home resident!

Hold True to Yourself

Holly

In the midst of all the turmoil, you will often feel as if your life has been turned upside down. Your family and friends may suffer from your inattentiveness, as your primary focus is on your parent's condition. Over and over, a million times a day, I asked myself what I could do to help my mother.

My initial reaction upon learning that mom needed skilled nursing was to adamantly defend my position of never placing my mom in a nursing home. I found that time with my family was confrontational and difficult. This was due to my digging my heels into the ground, and wanting to hear solutions other than placing mom in a nursing facility. As you may also experience, I felt as if I were all alone on a deserted island. I had a lot of soul searching to do, and my inclination was to be the guard at the gate for mom.

But my family didn't necessarily hold the same opinions as I held; they didn't want to handle the situation the same way that I did. As with many families, there was a lot of resistance from every corner whenever decisions needed to be made on mom's behalf. These decisions were also accompanied by plenty of guilt and unsaid innuendos. My family was a very close family, and I could see the closeness start to unravel, as we really didn't know how to react or what to do.

I felt that my family was not taking my opinions into consideration. I literally felt shoved aside. My mom had been a comforting and cohesive force behind our family, and she would not have wanted me or anyone else to break apart the strong family structure that she had spent her entire lifetime building. In retrospect, we were all doing what we thought was best for mom. I judged others too harshly, but ultimately, my family is my rock and I love them dearly.

What I Learned:

Sometimes family disintegration and disputes are unavoidable. Be patient and do your best to make it work. Respect each other's opinions, make an honest assessment, and avoid casting aspersions onto each other. You're in this together, be it good or bad, but the bottom line is recognizing each other's individualities and idiosyncrasies, and coming to a happy medium for your parent's well-being and happiness. As soon as you begin to forgive yourself, as well as others, it will pave the way to healing and gratitude. As for me, I now recognize that my family was always by my side, and no matter what, always wanted the best for mom.

Section Three

Accepting the Inevitable

Where Do I Start?

Holly

If anyone had ever asked me what one of my biggest fears was, it would have been placing a parent in a nursing home. Before I married, I told my husband that my parents would never be in a nursing home, and if they needed help, they would live with us where we would take care of them...and he wholeheartedly agreed. Sometimes uncontrollable circumstances happen and you must recalculate your course. After mom's first stroke, we had aides coming in, and emergencies and ambulation issues emerged. My brother lived in Buffalo and saw mom every day. They had a very close loving relationship. As I was living in Houston, my brother was my main lifeline as to what was happening with mom. Without him, I don't know what I would have done.

My husband and my son were my best support. They also loved my mom, and whenever they were with her, both of them were sensitive to her every need. My mother happened to be visiting us in Houston when she had her second stroke. My brother and I were told that she would no longer be safe living alone in her own home. Despite my pleas to get her to stay with me in Houston, she was adamant about returning to Buffalo. The second stroke resulted in loss of mobility; therefore, she needed more than one aide to assist her. All of her friends and family (aside from me and my immediate family) lived in Buffalo, and she had lived there her entire life. Unfortunately, safety and financial issues pointed to her need to go into a nursing home. We wanted to choose the best available nursing facility for her that was also close to her home, friends and relatives.

At this point, the nursing home journey begins and major decisions must be made... I found myself staring at a blank sheet of paper. It felt like I was in the midst of a major snowstorm knowing that something more ominous lay beyond this massive whiteout. The inevitable pain and fear that accompanies the decision to place a parent in a skilled nursing home was unbearable. It is a tortuous road of ups, downs, twists and turns, and sorrow and joy. I found joy in that my mom had survived her second stroke, and sorrow because of her fear and sadness in recognizing that a major change was about to happen for her. Once she started to decline, (and especially when she did go to live in the nursing home), she would often say she did not want to live the life that she was living. Truth be told, I wanted her to stay in this world with me, but I knew that she was ready to leave.

Remember, I promised myself and my parents that neither parent would go to a nursing home. As I'm sure many of you may wonder, weren't there other alternatives? The answer is "Of course"... but none that would ensure the safety and care that my mom needed and that we could afford. Having dementia, mom did not realize her limitations, and oftentimes she thought that she was perfectly capable of doing whatever she wanted to do, including driving.

I prayed to G-d and cried inconsolably every day, hoping that things would change. My mom was my confidante, one of my very best friends, the person that I called three times a day... but that all changed. I wanted my mom back, but now realize that she was my mom with a degenerative brain disorder, which diminished her ability to communicate.

What I Learned:

We all make promises and are truly sincere about keeping them. But life throws curveballs at you, and at some point, you must make decisions that are right for your loved one. When you first encounter what I call a life-changer, it may be difficult to clear your head. Step back and talk with your family, and come to the most viable solution given your set of circumstances. The safety of your loved one is the primary consideration, so remember that it's not about you, or what you may want. Consider enlisting the help of a geriatric professional, such as a Senior Care Manager, who can be truly invested in what your loved one is going through. A Care Manager can be of immense help, and may provide insight by offering better alternatives. Although family dynamics may get in the way, keep telling yourself that this is about what is best for your loved one. As for guilt, (there was plenty of that to go around), please try to be easy on yourself and your family. Know that you are doing the very best that you can. You have each other, and your parent would want you to get along and love each other. That would be their joy!

Guilt

Lauren

I remember the day as clear as anything. I had flown in from California to be by my mother's side while she was in the hospital. My mother had been admitted for a possible stroke, but as it turned out, she had just been dehydrated and overmedicated; overwhelmingly so, according to the hospital doctors. Prior to her hospitalization, she had been living with my dad for a few years in their two-bedroom apartment in the independent living facility.

Initially, we had aides to help my mom maybe two or three hours per day. However, once my mother's ability to walk became more and more limited, we upped the aide service, and came to rely upon a dependable group of aides (one at a time) to assist her with getting ready for the day, escort her to afternoon activities, and then help her get ready for bed. For a long while, my mother had aide coverage for about six hours a day, seven days a week (two hours in the morning, two hours in the afternoon, and two hours before bed). This was costly, but necessary, so that my dad was relieved of the responsibility of taking care of my mom. There were several aides who were exceptionally good with my mom, and they ended up being with her for years. (When you find a good healthcare aide, make sure you let them know that they are valued, and treat them as an integral component of your "family team!")

Although my mother had initially been very reluctant to move into independent living (she wanted to go home!), she did seem to adjust to her new environment fairly quickly. However, in the weeks prior to this hospitalization, her behavior had become very erratic and hard for everyone to deal with. No wonder - the more that we had complained about her depression to her geriatric psychiatrist, the more medication he prescribed, including several different psychotropic medications per day. The doctors in the hospital explained to me that the combined effects of all this medication resulted in the recent behavior that had become so difficult to tolerate — yelling, unreasonableness, interrupting my father's sleep, etc. It is my unsubstantiated belief that my mother's doctor had tried her on anything and everything as both a means to help her, but also primarily to get us (mostly me) off his back since I continually called him about finding a "solution" to her depression.

During this hospitalization, the medical staff took my mom off almost all of her medications. She started getting better right away, questioned why she was in the hospital, and was so happy to know that she would soon be going "home." Unfortunately, "home" was now going to be a room in the nursing home part of the same campus where her independent living apartment was located. It was decided by a majority vote of the family that because my mom had recently reached the point of immobility, it would be impossible to keep her in independent living, even with aides, unless we could afford healthcare service on a 24/7 basis, which, of course, we could not. Although I could not accept this, there was nothing that I could do. My mother was admitted to her room in the nursing home directly from the hospital.

When I met her in that nursing home room for the first time, she did not understand why she was there and not back in her apartment with my father. I can honestly say that day was one of the worst days of my life for so many reasons. First of all, remember the promise that I had made over and over to my mother and father when I was little, when we would go together to visit older relatives who were in a nursing home? I could not stand the smell of that place (cleaning agents with an undercurrent of urine); I could not stand the look of that place (so solemn and quiet, interrupted by the occasional scream, with sleeping people in wheelchairs lining the hallways); and I could not stand the feel of the place (abject misery). My promise back then was that I would never allow either of my parents to go into a nursing home, and that they would always have a place to live with me. I honestly don't remember my mother's response to my very sincere promise, but I am pretty certain that it was something benign, like "that would be nice". But here I was, many years later, standing in my mother's nursing home room, and there was no way for me to fix this. As my husband always says, "If one way to fix a problem doesn't work, there are always many other avenues to try. You just need to think outside of the box." Not in this case though. We had neither the ability to take care of my mother on our own since she could not walk, nor did we have the resources to pay someone to care for her twenty-four/seven while she was in my home, or back in the apartment with my father.

I honestly cried that day like I have never cried before. I begged and pleaded with the heavens for a miracle that would allow me to get her out of there. But it never happened. My mother was to spend years in the nursing home before passing away. It was never where she wanted to be, and never where I wanted her to be. I thought about her being there all the time.

If you are in a similar situation, and feel guilty about placing your loved one in a nursing home, remember my story, and know that you are not alone. Even though my family did what had to be done for medical, financial, and safety reasons, I must be honest and tell you that the guilty feelings are still with me. However, be consoled by the fact that this pit in your stomach will get better with the passage of time, as time presents you with the ability to step back and look at the reality of what was going on from a more objective perspective.

What I Learned:

Try to hang in there, and accept the fact that that you will undoubtedly feel guilty for a long time, regardless of what other people will say to comfort you. (Example: "You are a wonderful daughter and you should be proud of all the things that you do for your mother." In my head I would think, "How wonderful can I be? I allowed my mother to go into a nursing home!") Here's the bottom line: I am going to assume that you, like me, do not possess magical powers, and therefore, you cannot stop what has to be, no matter how painful it is. The key in all of this is to keep your loved one safe, and if the nursing home is the safest environment out of all your choices, then you have no choice other than to forge ahead with this placement.

Nursing Homes

Lauren

Nobody wants to be in a nursing home. Nobody wants his or her relative to be in a nursing home. However, the reality is that sometimes IT HAPPENS. Despite everyone's best intentions and well-thought out plans for the future, it happens. The nature of your loved one's illness can progress to the point that taking care of them in their home or your home, is no longer an option, unless you are a multi-millionaire and can afford round-the-clock care. For example, there are people who are forced to go into nursing homes because they are no longer mobile, like my mother. They must be lifted/transitioned via a Hoyer lift. (For those of you who do not know what a Hoyer lift is, count your blessings. It is a metal contraption with a sling chair that uses a hydraulic system to move people from place to place, such as a bed to a chair, or from a chair to the toilet. Whenever you see it in someone's room in a nursing home or the hospital, it is a sign that the occupant of the room can no longer walk, let alone take a few steps). The sight of a Hoyer lift still sends my stomach sinking.

As I related earlier, the day my mother was transferred from her independent living apartment to the nursing home (via a short stay at the hospital) is clearly memorable as one of the worst days of my life. I was strong for her. I hoped in my heart of hearts that her stay in the nursing home would be temporary, and that she would soon be back with my father in their independent living apartment. However, it was not to be, and no matter how much wishing or hoping or praying I did, she resided in the nursing home for over 5 years until she passed away.

Of course, all nursing homes are different to a certain extent. In my personal/professional experience, I visited facilities that were nicely furnished with great floor plans. There were some facilities that smelled, and some that didn't. In some nursing homes, everyone seemed "busy", while in others, the aides always seem to be grouped together talking, while the call bells kept ringing. Although the facilities are called nursing "homes", I have never seen a nursing home that bears much resemblance to my definition of a home. Regardless of what is outwardly going on, the reality is the same for every nursing home that I am aware of. Residents are primarily dependent upon the aides. Aides are usually underpaid, and sometimes their jobs do not come with any benefits. Their jobs are not easy, and oftentimes, there can be a "revolving door" of aides at the facility vs. consistent staff. Just as in all professions, there are some good aides and bad aides, along with some aides that are just OK. Without question, at some point in time, one of the "bad" aides is going to be on duty and responsible for your relative's care.

What I Learned:

- **Visit Frequently:**
  If the nursing home staff sees you around on a frequent basis, they know that you are involved and interested.

- **Be an Advocate:**
  Speak up, and continue to speak up on your relative's behalf if you see a problem. Do not be afraid that you will make things worse. While there is the possibility that this may happen, you must speak up. Your relative is probably in no condition, either physically or mentally, to advocate on their own behalf, so you must do so for them. Go up the chain of command if you must—from the aide to the Director of the nursing home. (Yes, I have done this!). If you are not the

"speaking–up" kind, I suggest that you hire a Senior Care Manager to be your resident's advocate.

- **Schedule family and friends to visit:**
  If you live out-of-town, try to schedule family/friends to visit in your absence. They can alert you as to any potential problems that they observe. They will also add credence to the notion that this is an interested, involved family that plans to stay on top of the level of care that is given to this resident.

- **If you and/or friends and family cannot visit frequently:**
  If at all possible, hire someone to visit in your place. This may be as simple as paying your family's next-door neighbor $15 an hour to go to the nursing home several times a week to report to you as to what is going on. Another alternative is to hire a "companion" service available from the many home health agencies that are now catering to the various needs of the senior population.

- **If you do not have the funds to hire someone to visit your loved one in your absence:**
  Check with the nursing home volunteer coordinator. Often volunteers will gladly visit residents of nursing homes if the residents have no relatives or friends in the area.

- **If your parent or relative can talk on the phone:**
  Call every day! It is so important to the nursing home resident to let them know that someone cares, and is always thinking about them.

- **Make friends with the staff of the nursing home:**
  It takes a special person to work in a nursing home environment. When warranted, make sure that the staff knows that you are appreciative of their efforts, either with a kind word or some special treat, such as candy or flowers.

- **Make friends with other families of residents:**
  I wish that I done this for my mother when she was in the nursing home. This friendship gives you a whole extra family of eyes and ears. For example, I did become close to another woman, Peggy, whose dad lived in the same independent living apartment complex as my dad. Our dads ate dinner together every night. (This was after her mother had passed away, and my mother was moved to the nursing home). She was local, and I wasn't. Believe me, Peggy kept me up-to-date on a frequent basis as to what was going on with staff, residents, etc. at my father's complex. If there was an immediate problem with my dad, and she could handle it, she did. I was so thankful for all her help and support, and to this day, we are still good friends.

  Remember, although this is not an easy time for anyone, what choice do you have? Use the above-mentioned suggestions to help you weather through so that you can monitor your loved one in the nursing home, even if you do live out-of-town.

The Search

Holly

Being more spiritual than religious, I turned to G-d and implored him to make everything better. I searched for answers that I knew I would never find. I always envisioned my parents being healthy and self-sufficient. But when serious illness strikes one or both of your parents, you may find that roles get reversed.... you wind up taking care of them and making important decisions on their behalf. I would have readily sold my soul if the exchange would have brought my mom and dad back to good health. Unfortunately, as we all realize once we reach a certain age, the fact is that you cannot always get what you wish for.

In the case of dementia and cognitive impairment, you may find your loved ones thinking that they can drive, they can walk, they can cook...they are perfectly fine and can take care of themselves. But they can't. They try to walk and then fall. They try to cook, and end up walking away from the stove without turning off the burners. You may see negative personality traits that were never in their nature. They may cast aspersions onto you and make you feel like you want to crawl into a manhole and cover it with a lid. Although you can intellectualize that it is their illness that is making them behave so differently, you cannot help but internalize the hateful remarks, which leave an indelible scar on your psyche. You want to counter their attacks, but you know that they would never say such things if they weren't ill.

So many nursing home residents say "I want to go home". Those five words will be forever embedded in my brain. My mother said them to me over and over again. Of course, she wanted to be in her own home and have her life back the way it was. But it was not to be. And your life cannot be the way it was either. Your mom and your dad may be physically present, but their illness has robbed them of any ability to give you answers, to provide you with comfort, to take charge of the holidays, and to do the million other things that you had always done together. This is a very hard truth to accept, and when I allowed myself to really think about it, I would feel overwhelmingly depressed. I wanted nothing more than to run away and pretend this was all a bad dream. If this happens to you, be sure to limit your pity party because all your energy must be focused on finding ways to help your loved ones move through their illness. This is not about you and how you feel! If you were fortunate enough to have the kind of parents that Lauren and I did (the type who loved you unconditionally, and were always there for you with support and encouragement), it is now time for you to give them all the help that they need regardless of how depressed or distraught you may be feeling.

Of course, the realization that a nursing facility is the best place for care for your loved one is monumentally painful. Once you make this decision, try to shield yourself from others who will judge you. My biggest fear in life was to have a parent in a skilled nursing facility and I **never** thought that it would happen. However, once you take a hard look at family finances versus the astronomical expense of around-the-clock aides, you will know that you are out of choices, and the nursing home is your one and only option. Nevertheless, this realization does not make you stop praying for a cure, or hoping to win the lottery, or fantasizing about inventing the next "must-have" pet rock-type sensation that will bring in millions of dollars in sales, so that you have the finances to fund other care options. The search for a panacea was endless.

What I Learned:

Whatever your beliefs, find a place of introspection. I asked myself if I was doing the right thing. I don't think there is any real answer. But we did what we needed to do to protect our parents. My hope is that senior care will improve in this country by providing better alternatives, such as eliminating the sterile hospital environment of most nursing homes in exchange for more homelike and familiar settings for our loved ones. Perhaps our aging population would be better serviced by legislation which would allow for Medicare/Medicaid to pay for in-home care, or State funding to reward nursing home aides based upon their job performance, or even federal funding to develop innovative solutions to improve quality of life issues for the elderly.

Communication is Key

Holly

Sometimes life twists you in unexpected and unplanned ways. It throws you completely off balance and turns your life upside down. As my mom gradually lost her ability to communicate, I started getting more and more lost. Trained as a speech pathologist, I felt helpless because I was always able to assist others with communication issues, but when faced with my mom's communication changes, I felt there was little that I could do for her.

Throughout my life my mom had loving and kind words for me. When her dementia progressed, a new communication of harshness and accusations surfaced, and although I knew it was the illness talking, her words caused me so much pain. One night I found myself sobbing uncontrollably while sitting in my car in the nursing home parking lot. I felt helpless and alone. Suddenly a guardian angel in the guise of a woman, whom I recognized as a frequent visitor to the nursing home, knocked on my car door and asked me to go for coffee. She saw my despair, and as we talked, I learned that she was in the same situation with her mother as I was with mine.

I realized that both my mom and I were getting lost; my mom in her dementia and me in my sorrow. I wanted my nurturing mom back. Lauren had gone through the dementia experience with her mom, and helped to bring me back to reality. I wanted to fix everything back to the way it was, but over time, I came to the realization that what needed to be fixed was my perception of reality, and the way I communicated with mom. My mom was the same mom, only with an illness and no matter how she was on a particular day, she needed me to be calm and understanding.

Communicating with a dementia patient can be trying to those who do not understand the illness. We all want to be heard and understood. We have our limitations and our fears. The same holds true for our loved ones with dementia. They are fearful because they know something has changed. They may not understand where they are or why they are disoriented, as oftentimes they cannot remember what occurred in the recent past. Their short-term memory is severely compromised.

Imagine yourself as a patient in a world turned upside down, totally different from anything you've known. You may feel misunderstood, talked over, confused, invisible and disrespected. You may lash out simply due to frustration and anger. People may treat you with unintentional disregard. Because your memory has been diminished due to your dementia, you hear "Don't you remember?" or "I just told you that."

In some cases, you may think your rights have been taken away and you are being treated like a child.

We communicate differently based on the situation and the people with whom we are speaking.

As the adult child of a dementia patient, my suggestions are as follows:

Be kind and be patient.

Speak slowly and clearly, and maintain eye contact.

Use simple concepts.

Don't overload with information.

Allow for response time, and don't hurry or push for answers.

Be agreeable and reassuring.

Don't be argumentative or confrontational.

Ask questions that may require a "yes" or "no" response or shortened response.

Simplify tasks so that they are not too complex to process.

Praise and compliment.

Eliminate distractions while trying to communicate, i.e. background noises, TV, etc.

Make memory books (i.e. familiar photos with captions) which may stimulate communication as well as meaningful memories.

Address by name, i.e. "Mom, do you want something to drink?"

Be respectful and compassionate.

Touching and hugging can be powerful communicators.

 Written information will help remind your loved one of an appointment, or answers to repeated questions. Written, as well as visual information (depending on the severity of the illness) are extremely helpful as they provide a permanent visual cue.

If a dementia patient could verbalize their wishes, here is what they might say:

Look at me.

Listen to me.

Be kind to me.

Care about me.

Open your heart to me.

Ask questions for me.

Show concern for me.

Be fair to me.

Don't be hurtful to me.

Don't disregard me.

Don't ignore me.

Advocate for me.

Don't judge me.

Make sure I look good.

Smile.

Don't yell at me.

And above all...please **value** me.

What I Learned:

Communication is not just about exchanging information. You must also have a keen understanding of the emotions and intentions of the person you are trying to help. Body language and focusing on what's really going on with your loved one is just as important as the words you use. The dementia patient's ability to process information has been diminished. While you are speaking, much of the message may be lost.

The key to effective verbal and non-verbal communication is multi-faceted and complex. To explore this issue more fully, there is a vast amount of information in reference books and on the Internet. Our main objective is to simply open your eyes to better communication styles that may be of help when interacting with your loved one with dementia. And most importantly, give lots of hugs and listen with your heart!

A Difficult Choice

Holly

I want to address family visits to the nursing home. It is not easy watching your loved one change due to dementia. It is not easy watching their inability to move, to feed themselves, to enjoy daily activities. And so many times I've heard people say that they want to remember their loved ones the way they were. They want their nana, their grandma, their mother back. But they are still here...just different.

Their illness has taken a toll on them, and just as a mother watches her children change and evolve into another phase of development, your loved one is changing and losing skills and memories and cognition, and entering into another phase of his or her life. It is important to remember that these changes are not their fault, and they can do nothing to stop it or make it better. Dementia is causing them to slowly lose the very essence of who they once were. They did not sign up for this, and they still love you, even if they cannot show it in the same way that they used to. Please do not abandon them, or hold off seeing them under the guise that you will visit once they "get better!"

A friend mentioned that her son and grandson had difficulty visiting her mom because to them, she wasn't the same. Her mom loved them both so deeply. Although they loved her deeply too, they wanted to remember her as she had been, because they just couldn't bear the pain of seeing her as she was in her current state. I totally get that. That reaction is so common because people don't know how to act or how to communicate, or perhaps they feel uncomfortable because they are reminded that they may one day be in a similar situation. Whatever their reasons, I accept that it is only human nature to avoid painful situations, and by no means should we judge others for making decisions that were right for them at any given time.

My brother, Alan, made the decision to visit my mom each and every day as a loving son and brother. The importance of his visits was immeasurable to both my mother and to me. They were also important in that the nursing home staff knew that he would be there daily to look in on mom. Some of my other family members also visited mom and their kindness touched my heart. As I lived out-of-town, my visiting consisted of daily phone calls when mom was able to communicate, and frequently visiting Buffalo to see her. These visits were never easy, and in fact, most times they broke my heart, but the visits were never about me and how I was feeling....it was about my mom and my love and respect for her.

If anything, my hope for the future is that families and friends orient and educate themselves about dementia. It's about love and acceptance, and overcoming your painful feelings and pushing through that barrier to embrace your loved one who needs you in their life so much.

For those patients whose families and friends have deserted them for whatever reason (it happens!), take some time out of your visit and spend it with a resident who needs human contact and compassion. It is so very sad to see patients who never have company, especially when family lives nearby. The question would be: "If you were in a compromised state, how would you want to be treated?" Wouldn't it be wonderful if your family treated you with love and kindness?

What I Learned:

Please don't discard your loved one. Nurture the relationship and be patient. Visiting may be a difficult experience for you, but it is one that you can live with. Instead of burying your head in the sand, you will gain so much from learning about dementia, and treating dementia patients with dignity, respect, love, and kindness.

Your loved one will gain even more from your visits. Even if you feel that your relative no longer even knows who you are, never underestimate the comforting effect of a lingering touch or a hand gently being held.

Loneliness

Lauren

Imagine how painful it is to pine for your mother when she is sitting right next to you. For me, it was horrible. I cried to myself over and over, and wished with all my heart that my "old" mother would come back to me. I knew that my mother was present on some levels.... I recognized her impishness in the smirk on her face when the nurse tried to tell her what to do, or when she told a clever joke, and I loved the winks that she always gave to my children.

Nevertheless, she was not the same mother that I had grown up with. I knew that at some point, I would have to reach the place where I finally accepted that the relationship between us would never be the same again. The woman that I had turned to for everything could no longer provide me with support, encouragement, or comfort. The person who knew me best of all now turned to me for these things. My mother did not have Alzheimer's, but it is clear that she was suffering from mild to moderate dementia. Her long-term memory was fairly intact, but her short-term memory was shot. Anything that you told her about the present day had to be repeated many times. She didn't talk as much, and couldn't really get into the paper or TV. We were still able to speak on the phone every day, and I know that she welcomed my calls. Oh, but there were so many things that I wanted to talk to her about, but couldn't! Mostly, I just wanted my mother to tell me what I should do about my mother, if that makes any sense.

How do you adjust to such a tremendous loss? I can't say that you ever do adjust, but I know that you must learn to accept the loss. It is not going to get any better no matter what you do, or how hard you pray. As a matter of fact, it will likely get worse. Acceptance comes slowly...I think it first comes as a cognitive acceptance, and much more reluctantly, it comes as an acceptance in your heart. It is accepting the slow demise of the personality of the person you love so much, and taking this new, very different person into your heart. My mother relished my visits, and I loved to see her. Sometimes I was scared that I would find her in worse shape than on my previous visit, but I always loved seeing her beautiful face. I never once thought about not visiting her, although I know that is the route that some people end up taking.

What I Learned:

If your loved one is no longer the same because of dementia, Alzheimer's, illness, or some other factor, don't forget about them! Encourage friends and relatives to visit too! Some people say, "I can't visit because it is too hard...I want to remember her as she was". They are just making it easier on themselves, and not on your loved one. Visiting is stimulation, and stimulation is good! Arrange family dinners and get-togethers in the family room of your relative's residence.

Always make sure that your loved one is a presence and a part of your life, and the lives of friends and family, no matter how difficult it is to arrange. Even if your loved one can't verbalize it, I believe that every person wants to know and feel that they are loved, and not forgotten!

Most importantly, remember to take pleasure in just being with your loved one. Don't think about what was; enjoy what is! Learn to take comfort in the small things, such as listening to music together, dancing to a familiar song, or even holding hands while sitting quietly. Relish the closeness and live in the moment.... you will not regret it!

Abandoned

Lauren

If you have ever spent any appreciable amount of time inside of a nursing home, I am sure that you have spotted certain residents who are off to the side, perhaps in a wheelchair or with a walker in front of them, but always alone. If you stop and talk to them, a few may seem appreciative of your interest, while others appear to be oblivious to your presence, or provide a non-response to your questions. They seem to be the same people that never seem to have visitors, and when you ask the nurses or aides about them, they confirm your belief. While the nursing home staff takes care of their basic needs, it looks like the rest of society has abandoned them.

I realize that there are residents of nursing homes who may not have any friends or relatives who are still living or who are capable of visiting. However, for the most part, I do believe that most nursing home residents do have some connection to another person or persons outside of the nursing home. If you know of someone in a nursing home, **never** assume that they have plenty of visitors, and therefore, would neither need nor want your company. Pay a visit yourself. In the scheme of things, it only takes a little time out of your schedule, while it could bring a lonely resident so much comfort.

Even when you visit your own relative in the nursing home, don't forget to pay attention to the other residents that you see around you. If the resident does not seem cognizant as to what is going on or is non-communicative, never underestimate the importance of a gentle touch on the arm, or your hand on their hand, or a soothing voice in their ear. Your simple gestures may be very comforting for the resident. No one, no matter what their situation, likes to feel that they are alone in the world. Your words or your touch could truly have a positive impact upon someone else's day.

If you know of someone in a nursing home who never seems to get any visitors, make sure that the social worker is alerted to that fact. (Don't assume that they already know; most nursing home social workers carry a very large caseload and can't know everything about everyone). The social worker could perhaps tap into volunteer organizations either within, or outside of the nursing home, to arrange for someone to visit that resident on a regular basis.

What I Learned:

While you are in the nursing home visiting your own family member, please remember to be aware as to what is going on with other residents. Don't forget to stop and say a few words to the person who looks up at you anxiously, or even the person whose head is bent down low. Hold their hand, and wish them a good day. It takes so little effort to be kind to another person. Homes are abandoned, things are abandoned, but human beings should never be abandoned.

Mirror, Mirror on the Wall

Holly

What would we do without a mirror? Some people cannot pass one without checking to see their appearance. It gives us a sense of knowing whether we look good or need to adjust our collars, brush our hair, or adjust our make-up. It's one of the ways in which we judge ourselves and gauge how others may see us.

What do dementia patients use as their mirror? Who assists them if their hair needs to be combed or their sweater is not on properly? Ultimately, they need to rely on people who have a healthy regard and respect for their best interests, whether it be their aides or their family members, or even just a passerby in the hallway, who upon noticing that a resident's shirt collar needs adjusting, just goes ahead and straightens it. However, if you look at the clothing, hair, etc. of some residents in a nursing home, you can see that this reliance on others to keep up physical appearances doesn't always work.

My mom always wanted to look her best, yet at some point in her dementia, she stopped looking in the mirror. One day while visiting, I found my mom sitting in the hallway with some other patients. She had pancake makeup all over her face, but it was on much too thick. When I approached one of the aides about my mom's appearance, she acknowledged that her makeup looked bad, but said that she didn't want to upset my mom, so she decided not to do anything about it. As a result, she simply left my mother in the hallway looking outlandish with that makeup on! I certainly didn't want to alarm my mother either, but I immediately took her back to her room and become her makeup artist.

As I was working on adjusting mom's makeup, I told her that I was giving her a "beauty treatment." Her face lit up, and she ultimately loved her "new" makeup when I showed it to her in the mirror. She looked great and I could tell that she felt special! The point that I'm trying to make is that it doesn't matter if your loved one is unaware of his/her appearance; if he/she loved to look good, then do whatever is necessary to make your loved one look as good as they can, simply because you know it is what they had always wanted` for themselves.

Another pet peeve of mine was going to the nursing home and seeing my mom's beautiful clothes totally destroyed by their laundry department. Since I lived out-of-town, I could not do my mom's laundry. The laundry department apparently "boils" the clothes, which make them shrink and discolor. I knew that if mom had been more cognizant, she would have been distraught to see her lovely outfits ruined. In retrospect, I should have paid a good laundry service or cleaner to take care of her clothes.

On another visit to the nursing home, mom was not in her room when I arrived. When I asked the aides where she was, they told me she was sitting in the front row at an activity being held downstairs at the nursing home. While I do acknowledge that I always asked the aides to be sure that they took my mom to activities that were of interest to her, rather than keep her sitting out in the hallway, I do know that this particular activity was not of interest to mom.

It is my opinion that the nursing home staff should do a better job of acknowledging and respecting their residents' core beliefs, and knowing what their hobbies and habits used to be, even if they are now dementia patients. For example, staff should know the resident's spiritual faith, or if they loved to watch the news on a certain channel, etc. Although I recognize that some of the things that residents liked to do pre-dementia may no longer be things that they can still do or even like to do, for the most part, familiar things can bring the dementia patient a great deal of comfort. I wish that I had told the staff (or they had asked me) about what my mom was like, as well as what she liked to do, prior to the onset of dementia. I feel sure that had they known more information about her, and exposed her to activities that were familiar to her, it would have made her feel more secure and less anxious in the nursing home.

What I Learned:

Most nursing home staff does not know anything about your loved one when they are admitted, other than their current physical condition, what medications they are taking, and how and when these medications are to be administered. As I have stated, I should have told the staff all about what mom was like prior to the onset of dementia. I could have been involved in making sure the staff knew how she liked to dress, how she liked her hair and makeup, and what activities she would have liked attending, as a guide for them to use when they were making personal decisions on her behalf. I could have helped the staff see her as a "whole person" vs. the dementia patient. As I recount those days, I realize that I cannot change my experience. However, hopefully you can learn from me, and be more vocal and proactive to ensure that the personal aspects of your loved one's daily care are in accord with what your loved one would want for himself or herself.

Postscript

Dr. Elliott Schulman, who is Lauren's brother and a neurologist practicing outside Philadelphia, very recently told us about a concept that was initiated at the Hospital of the University of Pennsylvania, in an effort to allow staff to get to know ICU patients as a "whole" person, and not just someone who is gravely ill. A standardized poster, entitled "Getting to Know You", is displayed in the patient's ICU room. Families of these patients are encouraged to contribute to the display. They can post photos of the person at work, with family, and engaged in activities that they like to do, along with lists of the patient's favorite foods and music, hobbies, etc. These posters allow staff assigned to their care to familiarize themselves with the patient's "life history." Elliott introduced the "Getting to Know You" idea during a staff meeting at Lankenau Hospital, located in Wynnewood, PA, which is the hospital that he is associated with. As a result, this program is now in place at Lankenau's ICU. **What a fantastic idea!** "Getting to Know You" posters should be in every room of every resident at assisted living facilities and nursing homes as a means to enable staff to really understand and familiarize themselves with the people under their care.

Advocacy

Lauren

I tried to act as my mother's advocate at all times. My mother could not always speak for herself, and I was more than willing to do it for her. I probably chose some ways to advocate that were not as effective as others. I wanted her to have a good life in the nursing home, which I guess is really an oxymoron. Let's just say that I wanted her to have the best possible life in the nursing home. There were times that I got angry at the staff when I shouldn't have, and other times that I didn't get angry at the staff when I should have. It is my opinion that any nursing home resident, even if they reside in what is considered to be the best nursing home in the area, needs an advocate to act on their behalf.

If at all affordable, I would also strongly recommend hiring an outside aide for at least several hours a day when family is not able to be with your loved one, for the following two reasons: 1) to give your parent special attention and; 2) to let you know what is going on "behind the scenes". Believe me, there always seems to be a lot going on. Suffice it to say that every facility that I am aware of continually has an aide shortage problem and always has some "bad apple" aides (along with some exceptional aides!). If you understand the underbelly of the nursing home - that is, who really wields authority on the floor, irrespective of titles - it may prove helpful to you at some point.

Another factor to consider when evaluating the need for an advocate for a nursing home resident is the idea that older people were brought up not to question authority, particularly the opinion of any doctor. In the view of most seniors, doctors are the "king" and their judgments should never have to be explained or challenged. I believe the opposite: ALWAYS QUESTION THE

DOCTOR! Make sure that you understand why they are recommending a particular course of action or medication for your loved one. NEVER assume that they always know what is best for your loved one. If the doctor, or anyone else for that matter, becomes angry because you are questioning his or her judgment, you have the wrong doctor and/or your loved one may be in the wrong facility.

What I Learned:

- Screaming or crying to get your point across is never a good idea. It just makes you look out of control and irrational.

- Act intelligently and calmly, and you will garner respect from the staff and administration.

- Think about strategy before you talk to the nurses, doctors, supervisors, etc. If you feel that there is an issue with your loved one's care, how can you best advocate? Do you ask for a staff meeting? Do you meet alone with the highest-up person in the facility chain-of-command who will meet with you? If you are not up to the task, do you hire a Senior Care Manager to advocate in your place? Each situation needs its own analysis to determine the best course of action.

- Do not sweat the small stuff! You cannot pick on every little thing that is going on that you don't like. Accept the fact that some issues will go unaddressed. You will never get anyone to hear you out on the important issues if you are constantly complaining about everything!

- Politeness and expressions of appreciation count! There's that old saying, "You can catch more flies with honey than you can with vinegar." For example, if you see an aide or a nurse doing a good job, speak up, tell the do-gooder and tell their supervisor. Everyone loves to be complimented on a job well done.

- Treats are appreciated. Whether your loved one is in the hospital, an assisted living facility or a nursing home, remember that the staff likes to be indulged with special food items, such as candy, donuts, bagels, etc. They will respond to your kindness!

- Try to set up a meeting with the social worker or head nurse on a regular basis, perhaps every week (even if done telephonically). They may not agree to it, but if they do, save all your concerns for the meeting (unless life threatening, of course), thereby eliminating calls during the week from you.

- In addition to a facility's requirements to follow federal and state mandates and safeguards, the facility will also have their own policies and procedures in place. Remember that there are some rules that cannot be bent or changed, particularly at the state and federal level, so don't waste your time arguing about them. (If you are unhappy about a state or federal law, take your concerns to the appropriate forum, i.e. your elected officials).

- Be innovative! Perhaps your ideas can make real change, such as starting a family support group within the nursing home if one does not already exist.

- Be creative! Perhaps the next time that a tour of a famous musical comes to town, you can arrange for the actors to come to the facility on their afternoon off, and perform an act or two for the residents.

- If you are a true advocate, do not accept the status quo! Keep thinking and keep dreaming about ways to improve the life of your loved one!

Section Four

Practical Advice

Are You a "Long-Distance" Caregiver?

Lauren

Don't think that you are not a caregiver because the person that you are providing "phone" assistance to lives out-of-town! Believe me, I know - I was that "phone" assistance person! Despite the fact that my mother and I did not reside in the same state, I was on the phone at least once or twice a week, sometimes more often, talking to the nursing home staff, including doctors, nurses, social workers, administrators, etc. trying to find out how to resolve a problem or just determining the status quo. (The facility would not agree to a weekly meeting with me; hence, the numerous phone calls).

Besides that, I was on the phone with my mom and dad at least twice a day. The rest of the time, I was **emotionally** invested in thinking about the fact that my mother was in a nursing home, mostly trying to figure out how to get her back to her own home, or even moving her to my home. Once I finally accepted the fact that neither of those scenarios were going to happen, I focused my time thinking about how I could make life better for her while she was in the nursing home. I came to visit as often as I could, which usually turned out to be once every 2-3 months. Logistically, the trip to Buffalo became easier once my family moved from California to Florida because of my husband's employment.

If you had told me then that I was my mother's caregiver, I would have said that I wished that I were, but that I was not. I envisioned her caregivers to be the staff of the nursing home, or the people that we hired as companions for her. In other words, the caregivers were the people who were physically with my mother. Now I realize that despite the geographical distance, I was an important and very integral part of her team, and I was most definitely one of her caregivers.

I was invested as a caregiver on all fronts—I knew exactly what was going on with my mom both physically and emotionally at any given time, and I knew what needed to be done and when it needed to be done. I handled every issue when it came up, (except for medical, as my family was fortunate in that my brother Elliott, a physician, handled all medical aspects). Most of all, I loved my mother and always wanted the very best care for her. I felt that I knew what she would want for herself.

Believe me, I am not negating the hard work and immense dedication of caregivers who have the physical as well as the emotional burden of caring for another. I applaud those of you who give of yourselves in such a profound way.

The only point that I am trying to make is that caregiving is a broad umbrella under which many of us fall. Recognize that if you are truly invested in the day-to-day process of making life better for someone who is physically and/or emotionally unable to care for his or herself, then you are a caregiver, and should take heed of the emotional and physical stress that you are under. I felt extremely stressed, but neglected to seek any relief for myself.

What I Learned:

- If you're a caregiver, seek out a support group. Support groups will enable you to meet with other people in a similar situation to your own. These groups can provide you not only with support, but also encouragement, advice, and the opportunity to vent.

- Local support groups should be easy to find on the Internet. However, if there are no caregiver support groups in your area, consider joining an on-line support group or starting a support group yourself by booking a room at a local church or synagogue, and advertising the date and time of the meeting in your local newspaper or community news.

- Respite for a caregiver is critical. Take some time off, both emotionally and physically, or you will soon find yourself in need of a caregiver!

Doctors and Other Professionals

Holly

Throughout my journey with mom, I've encountered some very good doctors and other professionals, as well as many inept and desensitized ones. I believe that most doctors and professionals working with a senior population strive to provide patients with the best and most compassionate care. However, maybe after practicing for a while, some have lost their enthusiasm for what they do. Perhaps they have been beaten down by the nursing home and health care system.

Many nursing homes are run by large corporations whose focus are on the quantity of patients and profits rather than the resident's quality of life. Fortunately, my mom was in a highly rated family-owned nursing home, and much of the staff was caring, and as attentive as time allowed. Nevertheless, nurses and aides worked long hours and the patient-to-aide ratio was below acceptability. In addition to patient responsibilities, the staff's time was consumed with paperwork and accountability to the administration.

As noted, even though this was a well-regarded nursing home, I still experienced a lack of honesty when I questioned the nursing home administrators about the fact that the facility required more care providers on staff in order to adequately care for its' residents. Their response was basically sending the message..." We're meeting the minimal requirements and we are not understaffed." However, the staff thought differently than the administrators. In private conversations with me, most of the aides and nurses stated that there needed to be more licensed nurses on staff; most were nurse's aides who were ill-equipped to deal with some of the medical concerns of the patients and their families. The staff also told me that some aides were poorly trained and overworked. It frustrated me when there was rarely anyone to speak with at the front desk for very long stretches of time; everyone was busy taking care of patients, doing non-clinical chores, or even talking on their phones for extended periods.

My mom had a fabulous doctor, but unfortunately, he was not able to treat her once she entered the nursing home. It's like today's hospitalists who treat you when you enter a hospital, while you have little connection with your own doctor, who has always treated you prior to your hospitalization. Imagine a patient with cognitive impairment who now faces a new doctor in the nursing home. I prayed that the nursing home doctor was a compassionate man. I did not know enough to ask if he was trained in geriatrics or certified by the American Geriatric Society, and just assumed that he knew how to relate to a dementia patient. That was my mistake, and hopefully I can prevent you from making the same one. He was abrupt and unfeeling, and told my mom that she wouldn't be returning to her home...the nursing home was her new home. He was the physician, and was using the new "reality therapy" in which you tell the dementia patient the absolute truth. Of course, my mom did not retain his biting comments and she quickly forgot what he had said. When I asked an aide about this new reality technique, she thought that it was very painful for most residents, and did not think this particular doctor worked well with the elderly patients. At that time, he was the doctor in charge of serving this nursing home community, and in my opinion, that was a reflection on the administrators; they should have been more cognizant of his skill set, including the traits of sensitivity and compassion, before they hired him to treat elderly patients entrusted to their care. This doctor spoke to me and my brother in front of my mom, telling us that she did not have much more time. That is when I fired him! Do not be afraid to question the doctor because if he or she is any good, they will be open to your comments, and can hopefully re-direct themselves.

Continuing education is crucial to the well-being of both the patient and the staff. This serves to update the staff on new and current practices relating to all issues, including dementia. This ongoing education should be required of everyone working in the nursing home...even the one in charge. An experience I had with my dad's supervising nurse in his nursing home was eye-opening. She told me that everyone had Alzheimer's (my dad did not), and she did not know the distinctions between Alzheimer's and the other types of dementia.

As for social workers, some are great and some are not. Engage them in conversation relating to their background and their philosophies, and question how they interact with patients and their families. Sometimes they are overloaded, but that is the administration's issue, and your loved one should be getting the fullest attention from the social worker. We had to ask for meetings and conferences, as there was little initiation on the part of my mom's social workers.

The activity director at my mom's nursing home was wonderful. She welcomed comments and suggestions so as to provide a more meaningful experience for mom. She asked about mom's interests and what she was like before her admission to the nursing home. That department shared with us important moments that they had with mom, and asked questions on how they could make it a more comfortable environment for her. Kudos to her and to other staff, who were exceptional, and went beyond just doing their jobs! My heartfelt appreciation goes out to staffers who made living with dementia a little easier for mom and for the family.

What I Learned:

I outlined my experience with staff and some of the incidents that you may encounter in your journey. My suggestion is to have a heart-to-heart meeting with the administration, the staff and the doctor before they approach your loved one. Do not give up your beliefs and your loved one's rights to those who may disagree with how you would like and expect your loved one to be treated. Their label of doctor, nurse, aide, etc. does not mean that they know more than you do regarding certain aspects of your loved one's care. Your advocacy is strongly needed, and there is no better person to advocate than a caring relative or friend who can be the voice of your loved one when they have lost theirs.

Explaining Dementia/Alzheimer's to Children

Lauren

If your mom or dad or close relative has been diagnosed with Alzheimer's or a disease-causing dementia, please do not put your head in the sand and think for one moment that your young children are not already aware that there is something different about their family member. For example, they will be clearly attuned to the fact that their beloved grandmother is no longer her same vivacious self. As their parent, it is up to you to help them understand what they need to know about dementia or Alzheimer's. For very young children, your explanation should be simplistic. As they get older, you can share more information. Listen to their concerns and answer accordingly. If they want more information, do not hesitate to provide it to them in language that they can understand.

There is a great deal of resource material on helping children to understand dementia or Alzheimer's that can be easily found online. I am not going to go over it here because I think that I can best help you by telling you how I handled things with my own son, Daniel, who is now an adult, but was about eight years old when my parents first moved into their independent living facility.

To give you a little background information, my son was very close to both my mom and dad. I brought him back to Buffalo to visit as often as possible, and when my parents were well, they would also come to visit us in California. Dan was probably three or four years old when my mother's physical health really started to decline. It was at that point that I began speaking to my parents every day by phone, just to check in to see how they were doing. Dan would often get on the phone and speak to them as well. It got to the point that Dan began dialing their number on his own to carry on private conversations with them, often without my knowledge. They adored him, and the feeling was mutual.

In all the years during which my parents were living in their independent living apartment, and even in the following years when my mother was in the nursing home, I never once had a conversation with Dan wherein I talked to him about dementia, or discussed the "hows and whys" of a nursing home. While I know that we talked about my mother all the time, these specific topics were never a part of our dialogue. In retrospect, I guess I assumed that because we visited my parents so frequently, he could see for himself that my mother was slowly declining on a cognitive level.

I also think that part of the avoidance on my part for never having "that talk" with him is that I was in some sort of denial about my mother's problems. I know that you are probably asking yourself as you read this as to how I could possibly be in denial since I was dealing with so many aspects of my mother's care. My answer is that I think I was engaged in a kind of magical thinking; that is, if I didn't have to say anything out loud about my mother's dementia to my son, then it simply wasn't true. This approach didn't serve me very well, and it certainly was not helpful for Dan. I can see now that I really let him down, and I am so sorry about that.

While writing this book, I spoke with Dan and asked him to recall his thoughts during the long period of my mother's decreasing mobility, accompanied by her increasing cognitive impairment. He told me that he remembers feeling an overwhelming sense of loss on so many fronts.... he missed my mother as she was before her illness, he missed their home where he had always visited, he missed our frequent family get-togethers at a favorite Italian restaurant. He was also scared. He told me that he recalls that he did not understand why his beloved "RoRo" (his name for my mother) was in a nursing home, because in his eyes, she clearly didn't belong there. He was also sure that it was the wrong place for her because he knew RoRo did not want to be there, and he knew that I did not want RoRo there.

Dan further told me that he had been afraid that his dad or I might have to go into a nursing home one day, and he often thought about what he could do to prevent that from ever happening. He also worried that he would have to go into a nursing home himself. I think that in some ways, the nursing home frightened him more than my mother's illness. It was such a big burden for a young boy to carry around. I am sure that I could have alleviated some of his worries if I had only been forthcoming and talked to him about what was really going on.

The good news is that it doesn't have to be this way for your family.

What I Learned:

I did my son such a disservice. I truly missed the boat on helping him through a very difficult life experience, which I will always regret. Please learn from my mistakes. If a family member or a close friend suffers from dementia or Alzheimer's, talk to your children about what is happening on an age appropriate level. Make sure they understand that you will always be available for them if they have any questions or concerns. Remember to explain the "hows and whys" of nursing home life. Knowledge is always power, while lack of knowledge can sometimes be much more frightening than the truth.

I also think that you can actually turn nursing home visits into learning experiences for your children in leading by example. If your children see you smile and visit a bit with residents that you pass in the hallway, they won't be frightened to do so themselves. Compassion and caring for others, even strangers, can be taught at an early age. I am proud to say that Dan learned this lesson well, and always had a kind word for other nursing home residents that he saw, whether he knew them or not.

On Medications

Holly

Medications usually carry benefits, but at times, they may also carry risks that can cause serious harm to the person taking them. All medications that are approved by the FDA have labels that tell us about the warnings and contraindications, if any. Some medications can cause adverse reactions, and knowledge regarding these reactions is essential. However, when your loved one has dementia, **they** cannot make the determination as to whether the medication that is prescribed for them will be harmful or helpful to them; it is the nursing staff that makes that call, and very often, the family is unaware of the ramifications of their decisions.

Some nursing homes are notorious for administering drugs to calm or simply "zombiize" the patient. When mom was admitted to the nursing home, we offered copies of her medical history, and lists of her medications and doctors. These medications were ultimately changed to conform to the medical plan administered by the nursing home doctor. After visiting mom, I wondered if her dementia was progressively and rapidly worsening because her moods were noticeably changing; she was lethargic at times and she would not eat...never knowing that her medications contributed to these behavioral changes. Doctors responded to family requests to help her by giving her different medications to appease us, as well as to appease the caregivers and staff. Medication switches were common, and caregiver and family frustrations were heightened.

Instead of giving sedatives and more medicine when a patient is crying and depressed, another solution could be spending time with them reminiscing and playing music, which was actually the best medicine for my mom. I believe that music is the ultimate medication in that it opens up emotional centers, and the rhythm and beat of the music generates more communication, and appears to create happiness for the patient. When I played Michael Buble's rendition of "Come Fly with Me", my mom would tap her feet and smile as if her world just opened up. I wanted my mom to feel better, to inhabit her changed world with greater ease and without pain.

My mom was in a good nursing home with caring staff. But in many nursing homes, although most of the staff wants to help, many are not taught how to interact with or treat dementia patients. I think they view all patients as one entity, and not as the unique individuals that they are.

Because of staff shortages, aides are thinly stretched. There is not enough quality time to spend with patients other than doing the basic chores mandated by their job descriptions. Wouldn't it be wonderful if the aide-to-patient ratios were high, and more time was spent addressing the psychological needs of their patients?

Some dementia patients may become irate and confrontational; often more exploration is necessary to determine the cause of that agitation. Medications play a role, but in my experience with my mom, undetected urinary tract infections caused severe agitation and mood changes.

Furthermore, aggressive behavior on the part of the resident often results in staff undertaking unnecessary measures, such as overmedicating, on their assumption that the resident is just "acting out". These unnecessary measures can prove to be very detrimental to patients. An example of this occurred to my mom's best friend, who was in a nearby nursing facility also suffering from dementia. One day, she became very agitated. Instead of using calming techniques, the staff rushed her by ambulance (without a winter coat) to the emergency room. Fortunately, her daughter was able to stay with her in the ER where she was kept for 11 hours. This was very cruel for a dementia patient who was not familiar with the surroundings. She was also given Haldol, which is a very strong anti-psychotic medication, and not meant to treat mental issues in dementia patients. In fact, in my research about Haldol, I learned that its use may increase the risk of death when used to treat mental problems in elderly patients.

When my mom's friend returned to the nursing home from the emergency room, she was incoherent, and never fully recovered from that incident. In this type of situation, staff should analyze whether the issue could be addressed in the nursing home, with the patient being calmed in a loving way, while still in their familiar environment vs. a chaotic, unsettling trip to the emergency room.

What I Learned:

It would be wise to consult a pharmacist or pharmacologist to assess the many drugs that are being given to your loved one. You have a right to another opinion, and quite frankly, not all prescribed drugs are necessary. Some drugs are counterproductive; while others may not be a good fit for your loved one's therapy plan. For example, over-sedating can cause falls and other side effects that are harmful to your loved one. You are not necessarily questioning the doctors' and nurses' decisions, but you are making sure that the drugs that are administered are necessary and beneficial. After all, the staff themselves would be the first ones to inquire as to the efficacy of any drugs being prescribed to their parent or loved one.

I also learned that we must find better models of care, and more creative ways to help dementia patients and their families through this insidious disease, without unnecessarily medicating/over-medicating them. We must do our due diligence on our loved one's behalf.

Sandwich Generation

Lauren

I was a member of the sandwich generation, a term given to a generation who simultaneously takes care of their elderly parents while also caring for their own children. When my mother first started having major problems with arthritis, my parents were living in their own home in Buffalo; I was living with my family in California, and my oldest child, my son Daniel, was just a newborn. In fact, my parents could not travel to be with us when he was first born because my mother was in the throes of a period of debilitating pain and could barely walk. As my mother's illness progressed and her pain became more difficult to manage, my parents' visits to California decreased, and my visits back to Buffalo increased. While my physician brother was taking excellent care of my mother by overseeing her medical treatment, I deemed it my role to make sure that she was comfortable and emotionally stable.

Over the ensuing years, I began making more frequent trips to Buffalo. Dan was still a baby and I would often take him with me. While there, I would help my parents as much as I could by running errands, investigating resources and programs that I thought my mom might benefit from, and providing my dad with some respite from shopping for groceries, doing the laundry, and especially helping to take care of my mom. (They refused to hire a cleaning service or outside help of any kind). Dan ended up developing a very strong bond with my parents. When I was back in California, I would speak to my parents by phone at least once a day. Dana, my husband, always supported my close interaction with my parents because he loved them and also knew how concerned I was about them.

When my parents ultimately moved into an independent living facility, my son was about 8 years old. During their first few years residing there, I felt that I could relax my vigil because they now had a medical support system right outside their front door, and all their physical needs were being met. As time went on, I saw the need to come even more frequently because my parents loved it when my son and I (and sometimes my husband) visited. These shared moments lifted their spirits tremendously and gave them so much pleasure.

My daughter, Jessica, was born when Dan was almost twelve years old. The logistics of traveling to Buffalo with two children, one an infant, absolutely made things more difficult all the way around. By that time, my father lived in his independent living apartment, which was a good half mile walk from my mother's room, as she was then in the nursing home. (Both the independent living apartments and the nursing home facility were under the same roof, so we did not have to go outside to get from one area to the other). My mom could no longer walk, and was experiencing early symptoms of dementia. During my visits there, I would be running all over the nursing home facility trying to talk to various staff members about my mother's care, while at the same time, attempting to care for a 12-year-old and a baby, all on my own. In contrast, when Dan was an infant and we went to Buffalo, my parents were living in their own home; my mom was mobile, and did not exhibit any signs of dementia. In those days, all of us were able to go out to dinner, see a movie, and visit with relatives and friends. My parents could care for Dan if I needed to go out, or just wanted a break. However, when circumstances changed, it became apparent that the only way my parents would get to see and know my daughter was if I brought her to them. That was the reason that I took Jess with me as often as I could.

I never thought that my mother would have to be in a nursing home, and my guilt was overwhelming (Remember the promise that I had made). In order to relieve some of my guilt, I felt that I had to make sure, first hand, that she was getting the best care possible. When I wasn't physically with her, I worried about her all the time. Although my father visited with my mother every day, I did not want him to feel that every aspect as to her care rested on his shoulders. Close relatives were consistent visitors, but long-time friends started coming less and less, until they finally stopped coming altogether.

By the way, to this day, I don't know why their visits stopped. I can only wager a guess. My opinion is that visiting my mother in the nursing home was depressing for them on two levels:

(1) my once vibrant, outspoken mom with the quick wit could no longer remember things, was much more subdued, and was sometimes confused, and later on, frequently confused; and

(2) they identified with my mother in that it brought home the reality that if my mother could end up in a nursing home, it might also happen to them. All I can say to that is **VISIT VISIT VISIT**! Get over yourself and understand that this is not about you—it is about helping a friend who needs your support and compassion!

But let me get back to the topic at hand...

As I have said, I felt that my physical presence was needed to oversee my mother's life at the nursing home on as frequent a basis as possible. My mother lit up when I came to see her. We played cards, we gossiped, we talked, and even if she was confused or couldn't remember, and I had to repeat stories over again, it was still wonderful to be with her.

Jessica was the one who suffered the most with my frequent Buffalo visits. When I was away, and I didn't take her with me, my husband would take her to the babysitter for the day so that he could go to work. When my husband was required to be out-of- town on business, which was a fairly common occurrence, she also ended up sleeping at the babysitter's until either my husband or I returned home. I did try to arrange my visits around holidays and school breaks so that at least my son could be in Buffalo with me. I knew that he loved being with his grandparents and they really loved seeing him. However, the reality was that I was also taking him away from his father and his sister. No matter what the scenario, my mind was **always** in two places at once, and I was constantly worried that I was neglecting my own family when I was with my parents, and vice versa.

Let's face it, membership in the sandwich generation is just in the cards for some of us; there is no way around it. As difficult as it was, I tried to view it as a blessing in that my parents were alive, and I could still visit and have meaningful times with them.

What I Learned:

If you find yourself in this "club", I do have some advice for you. Accept the fact that no one can be two places at the same time. Focus on being with whomever you are with physically, and try not to dilute the experience with guilt and stress. Do the best that you can do, which is, I know, easier said than done. Try very hard to surround yourself with supportive people...and don't be afraid to let them know how you are feeling emotionally. I made the mistake of keeping a lot of my feelings inside because I thought that no one would understand my turmoil. If you do not have supportive people in your life, either join or start a support group for other people who find themselves in your same situation. Lastly, remember to be kind to yourself! We can often be our own worst enemies!

Abuse

Lauren

Abuse can happen in nursing homes, just as it happens in schools, workplaces, within families, or basically anywhere. When you have a loved one in a nursing home, it is better to take a pro-active stance regarding abuse. In other words, always be on the lookout for signs of it! Don't put blinders on and believe that your loved one will never be abused because they are in the "best" nursing home, or because you are always visiting, or because the staff likes you, etc.

Obviously, do suspect abuse if your loved one has unexplained injuries. Conversely, don't ever assume that there is no abuse simply because you have never seen any signs of unexplained bruises or black and blue marks. Remember, some signs of abuse are not so obvious. Subtle indications of abuse may include any unexplained change in mood or behavior, such as becoming withdrawn, angry, non-responsive, or going from having a good appetite to no appetite. Be aware that neglect is also a form of abuse, so be on the lookout for signs of poor hygiene, such as unwashed hair, as well as other more apparent hints, like the fact that the resident is still wearing pajamas in the afternoon, or is wearing dirty clothing.

Sexual abuse and emotional abuse can also occur in nursing homes and long-term care facilities. However, these types of abuses may be difficult to detect in residents. To begin with, some residents suffer from varying degrees of dementia or Alzheimer's or some other type of cognitive impairment that precludes them from actually verbalizing that they have been (or are being) abused. However, even if a resident is capable of telling you about an abuser, he or she may be very hesitant to do any reporting for fear of backlash, as nursing home residents are so dependent upon the staff for all of their care.

Another consideration to be aware of is that your loved one may be abused by another resident of the nursing home or assisted living facility. I know for a fact that this can and does happen based upon my own experience as a Senior Care Manager.

If you suspect abuse of any kind, what do you do? Of course, we have all seen the commercials on TV alerting us as to which lawyer to call "if you suspect that your loved one is the victim of nursing home abuse". Investigating abuse in a nursing home or any other long-term care facility is not merely as simple as making a phone call to an attorney.

The first thing to do is to talk to the administration, as all nursing homes and other long-term care facilities should have written policies that mandate that they address your concerns about your relative's care. Your next call should be to file a complaint with the appropriate state agency, such as Adult Protective Services. All 50 states in the U.S. have Adult Protective Service agencies. Additionally, all states are required to have a long-term care ombudsman program to both advocate on behalf of residents, as well as to address the problems and concerns of residents in nursing homes, assisted living facilities, etc. Therefore, in addition to contacting Adult Protective Services, you should simultaneously call the police and the local ombudsman to investigate. The number for the local ombudsman should be publicly posted at your loved one's nursing home or long-term care facility. Lastly, you may want to contact an elder law attorney to determine your loved one's legal rights in an abuse situation.

Here is my story about what happened when my mother was suspected of being the victim of abuse. My mother spent over five years in a nursing home on the same campus where my dad resided in independent living. My dad passed away several months before this alleged abuse incident took place. At the time, my mom was verbal, with moderate dementia. My mom and I were still having telephone conversations every night. We were paying for outside aides to be with my mother for several hours every day, and for longer periods on the weekends. For the most part, the same rotation of aides had been taking care of my mother for years.

One day I received a hysterical call from one of these aides. She informed me that she had been accused of hitting my mother. Two nursing home staff members allegedly witnessed my mother being hit by her and had reported it. The aide told me that the alleged witnesses were the very same people that she always had problems with; she felt that they were slow in responding when my mother needed to go to the bathroom or wanted to go to bed. (By law, since the aide did not work for the nursing home, she could not operate the Hoyer lift, which was necessary to use in order to move my mother from place to place, since she could no longer walk. Therefore, my mother's aide had to call the aides who were on duty at the nursing home to make these transitions for my mother). My mother's aide contended that she would never hit my mother. Her story was that the staff aides were seeking revenge for the numerous times that she had reported them for failing to perform their duties.

I was shocked, and certain that this aide would never hit my mother. My brother and I spoke, and he concurred. We were completely convinced of the aide's innocence. We were angry that the facility had suspended her right to work with any of their residents until the matter was resolved via an administrative hearing. My mother, when questioned, said that she had not been hit, nor did she show any outward signs of being hit. We wrote a joint letter to the facility in support of the aide, asserting that we both knew that she would never harm our mother.

Several weeks later, there was an administrative hearing where both sides had the opportunity to tell their story. The hearing officer ruled in favor of the staff, and permanently barred the aide from working in my mother's nursing home. At the time, my brother and I were very sad to lose this woman as my mother's aide. We trusted her implicitly. When my father was dying in the hospital several months before this incident, and we were waiting to get him into hospice, she was the only person that we trusted enough to sit by my father's hospital bedside one night, so that we (my brother, my husband and myself) could get some much-needed relief from the twenty-four/seven shifts that we had put ourselves on to prevent my father from ever being left alone.

When I told my brother that I was writing this book with Holly, he and I talked about this alleged abuse incident. He urged me to put in a section addressing abuse in long-term care facilities, and to specifically talk about what happened to us. During this conversation, we decided that we had made a mistake in writing the letter in support of the aide; we did not know for certain whether or not my mother had been hit, as we were not present and did not personally witness the incident in question. Although my mother bore no physical signs of abuse, and never complained about being abused, we should have erred on the side of caution, and not taken any position as to the private aide's guilt or innocence.

What I Learned:

I will never know for certain whether or not my mother's private aide hit her. I still believe that she did not. However, in retrospect, I will tell you that instead of being angry that this aide was prohibited from servicing clients until her guilt or innocence was determined, I should have been happy that there was a system in place to safeguard the helpless, and that my mother was potentially protected from an alleged abuser. If you suspect abuse, always err on the side of caution! Make sure that you report it, and that your report is shortly followed by a thorough investigation by the administration and the appropriate authorities. If you are wrong, you are wrong. Conversely, if you are right, you will have protected someone who is more than likely incapable of protecting themselves. In the scenario that I have relayed, my brother and I should have recognized that our only duty was to do absolutely everything in our power to ensure that our mother was protected vs. trying to protect the aide.

If a similar situation ever happens to you, you have my sympathy. Unlike me, stay focused on your one and only priority, which is to always act in the best interests of your loved one.

Hospice

Lauren

I am fairly certain that, for most people, the term "hospice" carries a negative connotation. Simply stated, most people associate hospice with imminent death. However, you should know that a person may be under hospice care for six months or longer before they pass away (or get sent home). Regardless of the length of time that a patient receives hospice care, once in hospice, in most instances, the goal shifts from "curing" to a focus on comfort and quality of life.

Hospice provides services in a variety of settings, including a hospice facility, private home, hospital, nursing home, or an assisted living facility. Although my Dad died in hospice only five hours after being admitted (after several weeks in the hospital), I was impressed with the hospice staff who were there to greet me and my brother at midnight, when our Dad was brought there by ambulance. I believed them when they promised to take good care of our Dad, who was not conscious. Once the staff got him settled into his room, they brought us in, and I noticed right away that my Dad actually looked much more comfortable than he had looked in his hospital bed. I know that the hospice staff listened to us when we talked about our Dad because the TV was turned to the Weather Channel, which was one of his favorites. I left feeling assured that he was in good hands, and believe me, I wouldn't have left if I hadn't felt that way. For the ten days prior to the move to hospice, my brother, my husband and I had taken shifts so that at least one of us was with my Dad at all times, sitting in a chair in his hospital room next to his bed. I will never be able to thank my husband enough for his love, support and comfort during this horrible time. He left his sole practitioner business completely unattended, and was there to relieve me and my brother at our father's bedside, without ever voicing a complaint. He helped with funeral arrangements, and made calls to friends and family on our behalf. He was my rock; I don't know how I would have made it through the experience of my father's completely unexpected death without both my husband and my brother by my side.

Hospice provides services via a team approach (Doctor, nurse, social worker, chaplain, home health aides), and access is available 24 hours a day, 7 days a week. Their goal is to make the patient as comfortable as possible through the use of medication (to control pain and nausea, for example), to provide medical supplies and equipment (such as a hospital bed, wheelchair, etc.), and just as importantly, to provide emotional support to both the patient and to the patient's family.

My father-in-law used in-home hospice services, and again, the staff was wonderful. They were supportive yet unobtrusive, and were always responsive to his every need, as well as the needs of the family. I am thankful that hospice is there if needed, and support their services wholeheartedly.

What I Learned:

If it comes to the point of needing hospice services, don't be afraid; just do your research! What you will learn is that hospice is not a bad word. Prior to having any experience with hospice, I viewed it as the dreaded call that I would have to make once all hope was gone. Turn this thought around, and take the focus off how you feel! Be brave and open enough to embrace hospice, and accept and understand that hospice is a wonderful gift that you can give your loved one, as it will ultimately assure them the dignity of dying in comfort and at peace.

Who Cares for the Caregiver?

Holly

A caregiver doesn't always ask for help. Their thoughts are: "We're invincible; we'll take care of everything." It's not in our nature to have someone else manage the many challenges that may arise for our loved ones. We don't want our layers and layers of protective insulation to come apart and let the world see that we may not be as strong as we pretend to be.

It is only when caregivers recognize that they are not all-powerful...that one simply cannot be in control of everything and still do a good job...that half the battle is won. The other half of the battle is to learn how to DELEGATE!

Initially it was very hard for me to give up control because I had always promised to take care of my loved ones, and I also believed that I was the one person who knew what was best for them. Over time, I eventually accepted that there were other caregiver personalities in my family who also wanted what was in the best interests of my relatives.... even if their plan was not in sync with mine.

As you take on the role of the caregiver, be it either a physically present caregiver, or a long-distance caregiver, the question that must be considered is who will care for you? The best answer is that YOU must. If you don't take care of yourself, you won't be good for anyone or anything else. You'll slowly start to unravel, both mentally and physically, because of your overwhelming feelings about the situation and your perpetual state of exhaustion. You will be short-tempered with friends and family. You'll start your self-hate talk.

Well, I am here to give you some advice: Don't wait until you are completely wiped out mentally, physically, and emotionally before you take some positive steps on your own behalf. I've been there, and you don't ever want to be there! Enlist the assistance of your best friends, your relatives, and anyone who was a friend to your parent to help you out. If this does not provide you with some relief, then find a Senior Care Manager and/or even a social worker at the facility to assist you in your role as a caregiver.... just as long as you find someone with whom you can trust and communicate, who understands the situation, and who has the knowledge and experience to provide you with support and concrete assistance.

You also need to get grounded because when your loved one has dementia. It's a roller coaster ride each and every day. You want to get off the ride, and take them with you to safer ground, but that's not going to happen. Along the way, they may hate you, they may say things you've never heard them say before, and they may seem to be a complete stranger in your loved one's body. My experience was that I did not want to talk to anyone else about the emotional and physical drain that I was experiencing as a caregiver. The end result is that I turned inward and shut out the world. I didn't want others to see that I needed help. Don't be a martyr like I was!

What I Learned:

Talk to someone who will care for you...talk to someone who will say they understand...talk to someone who will just hug you and listen. Then find someone who can run errands for you, and can periodically take your place for lengthy visits to your loved one, so that you can get some relief to rest and recharge. This break will enable you to come back as the best caregiver that you know you are. Have a plan for several alternate caregivers to ensure that there is always someone to turn to for coverage. (If you want to skip this last step, hire a Senior Care Manager to handle everything, and let them advocate where necessary on behalf of your loved one, as well as be the lead in arranging, hiring, and checking up on substitute caregivers).

You give because you want to give. If you don't take care of yourself, you will have little to give to anyone else. Be sure to be good to yourself. It will be helpful for all caregivers if you create and follow a Care Plan, which is something that I did not do, but wish that I had done. A Care Plan is a written document that sets out goals to help your loved one (goals may be set out under categories such as "Medical" or "Social"), in addition to recommendations as to how to achieve each goal. For example, one of your goals may be as simple as having all substitute caregivers write into a logbook so that when you visit, you can read what has been going on in your absence. Recommendations to achieve this goal may include: 1. Holding a conference call with all caregivers and instructing them as to what information you would like logged, i.e. "Did my mother seem depressed when you were with her today?", "What stimulating activities did you do with her to try to get her out of her depression?", etc.

Share the Care Plan with all caregivers so that everyone is on the same page with respect to caring for your loved one.

Plan for unforeseen circumstances. Ask yourself "what if" scenarios, and be proactive in establishing viable solutions that work in the best interests of your loved one. Take long stretches of time off every week. If that is accomplished, as hard as it is, you will be able to recharge yourself so that you can make each day a better day for your mom or dad, as well as for yourself, the caregiver.

Wishes

Holly

We all tend to avoid uncomfortable conversations. Nevertheless, it is wise to have ongoing dialogue with aging parents to ascertain their wishes in the event that at some point in the future, they are incapable of making their own decisions. Hindsight is 20/20. I wish I had sat down with mom when she was well so that we could have discussed what she wanted for herself if she became ill, and what she would expect if we could not safely take care of her. Unfortunately, this particular conversation never happened.

If I would have had some idea as to what mom's wishes were, perhaps all or most of the ensuing chaos associated with planning for her after her last stroke could have been avoided. If I had not been afraid to ask the questions, I know without a doubt that mom would have talked to me about anything. Mom was smart and organized, and even left a written note for my brother and me to open after she was gone. (In this note, she told us that she loved her family and had enjoyed a fulfilled and happy life).

As I previously told you, when I was growing up, I made a promise to myself and to my parents that there would be no nursing homes in their future. I told them that if they ever needed help, I would either take care of them in my home or in their home. Maybe you made the same promise. Then reality hits, and a nursing home placement turns out to be the only viable option. As hard as it may be to accept, you are not breaking your promise when their safety is at risk. To give you some background, when my mom was in the early stages of dementia and it became clear that she needed some assistance in her home, we hired an aide to stay with her. My mom did not want the aide around because she felt she didn't need help. She insisted that she could cook, drive and be on her own, but that was her dementia speaking. This was a difficult time. My mind was always focused on Buffalo, while I was physically in Houston working and taking care of my family. After my mom's second stroke, which happened while she was visiting us in Houston, we were admonished that it would be considered elder abuse if she were living alone in her condition. I was terrified about what the future held. Meanwhile, my mom, having no concept that she was permanently incapacitated, just wanted to return to Buffalo. She absolutely refused to stay in Houston. However, several days later, while in rehab, she had a lucid moment and told me that she would be willing to try nursing home care in Houston because she accepted that she was now entering another phase in her life. I vividly recall my joy and relief in knowing that at least we now had a plan! Unfortunately, my relief was short-lived, because the next day she had no recollection of our conversation, and demanded in no uncertain terms that I get her back to Buffalo. If I had only known when she was well what she would have wanted me to do if and when she became incapacitated.

I think most families, like my family, do not have "that conversation" with their loved ones. As a result, when these all-important decisions about the future of a loved one need to be made quickly, it can become a tug of war amongst the best of families.

After we placed mom in the Buffalo nursing home, I recalled how mom managed with my dad when several years earlier, she had to place him in a nursing home after his strokes and the onset of post-polio syndrome. His speech had declined and he was unable to walk. My mom visited him every day and took great comfort in knowing that he was safe and close to home. I was now making the very same choice for her based upon where I thought she would be the safest, and where family and friends could easily visit. When I thought about it that way, I knew in my heart that she would understand and forgive me.

However, I wondered if I could ever forgive myself for my decisions.

What I Learned:

Never say never! What happened to me can happen to you. Make plans, research, and ask the hard questions in a family discussion with your loved ones who are aging. There may be disagreements, but it's better to lay the cards on the table and have a heartfelt and honest conversation about the "what ifs". This isn't about pride or who has control...it's about your loved one and designing the best care plan for them.

Section Five

Reflections

Where Do We Go From Here?

Holly

It's over...Mom has gone to a more peaceful place. The chaos, the heartache, the uncertainty has left me numb. But how do I proceed? After the illness, the nursing home...how do you get back to you? When this final and dreaded event became a reality, I had to ask myself that question.

My answer is that you can never get back to the "you" you once were. Everything seems altered. You can never have the same conversation, you can never hold your loved one close, and you can never hear their soothing words and feel their touch. At that time, I felt that I was no longer anyone's child, and that my identity had changed. But you soon realize that you will always be your parents' child, and your mom and dad will always be your parents. Not even death can change that. I think that one of the hardest realizations that I had to face is that there would never be anyone who would be able to provide me with the same kind of love and concern that I experienced from my parents throughout my entire life...that unconditional, ever-constant, taken-for-granted love was gone. I remember my cousin telling me that she felt like an orphan after both of her parents passed away. I now know that feeling, and I did let myself wallow in that for a time. However, believe it or not, the passage of time does gradually soften the pain.

After you are able to finally stop crying, how do you find your way back to the "new" you? You have gone through so much. It is now time to surround yourself with family and friends so that you can be helped and supported on the road to healing. You may want to enlist the help of a professional or someone who can be objective. It takes time. It's been several years since my mom has left this earth, and I can say that I never got back to where I was, yet I've grown into a different, stronger person. Perhaps G-d knew where to take me, and answered my prayers as to where to go and what to do after mom passed away.

What I Learned:

Although it is a cliché, life does go on. There has not been one day that I haven't thought about my parents, as well as other loved ones that are now gone. I want them back, and there are times (especially certain holidays) when I want my life back to the way it was. You may feel the same way, but I would say to you what I continue to say to myself. You must cherish the present and be hopeful for a promising future. Where do we go from here? It's really up to us to decide on which path we choose to proceed. My hope for you is that it is a path of positive change and serenity.

Your Life Will Change

Holly

If someone had forewarned me before my mother's illness that my life would change so drastically, I would never have imagined the cascade of losses that I ultimately experienced. During my mother's illness and after her death, I not only felt the very real significance of her loss, but I also, quite unexpectedly, sustained the loss of my relationships with many family members that I had once been very close to. I soon grasped that their strongest tie to me was through my mother, who had been the only remaining sibling out of a close-knit family of four sisters. Once my mother was no longer able to host the family get-togethers and impromptu dinners, it felt like my family also gradually loosened their ties to me. It's like my mother was the tight knot who kept the family bound together, but once the knot was gone, the rest of the family veered in other directions, and ultimately went their separate ways.

You should be prepared to lose some family connections if your loved one was the person who held everyone together. No one stepped in to pick up where my mom left off, and I seemed to be the only person who was even interested in trying to keep our family close. I learned that not everyone is ready, or even wants to go back to some semblance of the way things used to be.

Several days ago, it was an anniversary of my mother's passing. I honored her by baking her favorite cookies and lighting a candle in her memory. It still seems so surreal. There is no timeline for healing, but I will say that the intense pain has diminished although the sadness is still here. Lauren asked me how I was that day, and my response was that it wasn't so bad. That being said, another friend saw my tears and sadness, gave me a hug, and told me that it would be ok. And it was...and what I would say is that the concern of friends, and the hugs and the assurances that everything would be ok, were the best and most comforting acts of kindness that I received that day.

What I Learned:

So, your life **will** change. **Family dynamics change.** Stop and remember the wonderful person your loved one either is or was, and reflect on the people who still surround you with their open arms and acts of kindness and love. And if their arms are not open, don't be afraid to extend yourself to give them a hug out of kindness and love. This will lead to the path of healing and wellness.

Grief

Lauren

During the years that my mother was in the nursing home, my gregarious, joke-telling dad was in very good health. In fact, as far as I know, he had been in good health for his entire life except for a bout with prostate cancer about 5 years before my parents moved into their independent living apartment. His cancer diagnosis was very frightening for all of us, but my brother (a doctor) reassured us that prostate cancer is very treatable if caught early (as in my father's case). My father's oncologist recommended that he undergo a course of radiation treatments, which he endured with little difficulty. Thereafter, my dad made a smooth recovery. Although he did start having problems with his knees in the last few years of his life, he made a great transition to an electric scooter for long distances, and loved to travel all over the campus where he lived. On our visits to Buffalo, Dan would hop on the scooter with him and off they'd go, both happy as clams!

One day in January 2003, I was talking with my dad in the early morning. He complained of not feeling well and told me that his arm was very swollen. I called my brother who told me to contact the front desk at my father's facility, and instruct them to call an ambulance for him. The emergency room doctors were in touch with my brother after examining our dad, and told Elliott that they were admitting him. They said that my dad had developed a staph infection in his arm because of an untreated cut on the underside of his arm. Holly and I have a close friend, Ellen, who still lived in Buffalo at the time. Ellen went to the emergency room to check on my dad as he waited to be admitted, and reported that he was in good spirits. In his initial weeks in the hospital, I visited my dad several times. He seemed very upbeat, and received a lot of company. However, the infection was still not under control; it appeared to be resistant to all the antibiotics that the doctors were trying. Still, my dad remained optimistic and hopeful that he would soon return to his apartment in independent living. I talked with him every day, and after a few weeks in the hospital, I began to notice that he seemed to be lethargic when we spoke. I was not unduly alarmed; I just thought that he was more tired because he was so inactive in comparison to his usual routine. The doctors never alerted me or my brother (to my knowledge) that our dad's health was declining. A day or two after I first noticed his lethargy, I received a call from a friend, who was the daughter of my dad's good pal from independent living. Her entire family was concerned when my dad initially went into the hospital and visited him regularly. During our call, she mentioned that my father seemed to be asleep during her last several visits to him. My dad was sociable and loved company; this was unusual for him. She thought something was not right.

My husband and I flew into Buffalo within a day or two of this call. I tried to wake my father up, but he wouldn't wake up, even for me. I could tell right away that something was different. We met with his doctor who told us that my father's kidneys had begun to fail and he did not think that my dad was going to make it. Even though my dad was in his 80's, this was a total shock to me and to my brother...our dad was full of life and had not even been ill in the days or weeks prior to this hospitalization. My brother flew in the next day, and the three of us (myself, my husband and my brother) just hugged and cried in the hospital hallway outside my father's room. I was not giving up though; I was convinced that I was going to will him to live by sheer force of my thoughts! The nurses told us that even though he appeared to be unconscious, he could hear us, and urged us to talk to him. My brother later told me that he talked to our dad to bring some closure for himself. I, on the other hand, talked to him because I thought that I could bring him out of his unconscious state. I carried on an almost endless one-sided conversation

126

during which I told my dad important things, as well as unimportant things. Even as I watched TV in his room, I would explain what was going on in the news or TV shows, as if his only problem were that he could no longer see. I held his hand, I wet his lips and I stroked his arms. Despite our diligent 24/7 vigil, my father never recovered. Aside from one meaningful short rally, he remained unconscious for over a week, until he passed away in hospice hours after we moved him there. As I noted, up until the week prior to his passing, his death was completely unexpected and hit me like a ton of bricks.

In contrast, I felt that I was prepared for the eventuality of my mother's passing. At the time of her death, my mother's life had been compromised by illness for more than ten years, and she had been in the nursing home for over five years. My mom was also in and out of the hospital regularly for various issues. About five months after my dad passed away, she was admitted to the hospital for dehydration. She had basically stopped eating, and the doctors were talking to us about inserting a feeding tube in the very near future. I arranged to have a small refrigerator ready to place in her room when she returned to the nursing home from this hospital stay, which I planned to stock with ice cream, one of her all-time favorite treats. I reasoned that it was better for her to eat something, even if it was ice cream, rather than nothing. Surprisingly, her doctor agreed. After spending several days with her while she was in the hospital, the doctors told me that she was scheduled for discharge within the next few days, so I felt comfortable leaving her and returning to Florida. The day after I got home, I received a call from my brother, who had just spoken with our mother's doctor. Apparently, she had taken a sudden turn for the worse and things did not look good. The doctor urged us both to come back as soon as possible. My brother was able to fly in that same day; I was not able to get a flight until the next day. My brother called me when he arrived at the hospital to tell me that he did not think that our mother would make it overnight, but I urged him to tell her that I was coming. When I arrived, my mother was just hanging on. I think that as soon as she heard my voice telling her that it was OK to let go, that is exactly what she did. She passed away shortly after my arrival.

In one year, five months apart, I had lost first my father and then my mother. I was now an orphan. The unthinkable had happened. After all those years of asking myself how I would ever be able to handle it when something happened to one of my parents, I now knew. I had to walk through the grief and carry on, just as you must do when the inevitable happens and your loved one passes away. Whether you are completely unprepared for the news (as I was with my father) or mentally ready for the news (as I thought that I was for my mother), the devastation (at least for me) was still the same. Both deaths made me feel completely alone, even though I wasn't. I had my family and good friends around to comfort me, but I felt that there was no one who could comfort me; I was inconsolable. My husband was absolutely supportive, (remember, he had stayed with me and my brother throughout our vigil at the hospital with my father, and even took his own shifts by my dad's bedside), but I was in my own world.

After their respective deaths, I kept looking for signs that my mother and father were trying to contact me, but there was really nothing. I saw hidden meaning into everything; after my father died our home alarm system kept going off for no reason, and I was sure it was a signal from him. I was grabbing at straws to maintain some type of physical connection, but to be honest, I have never really felt either of their presences near me. I still wish that would happen. I think that it took me a good year before I stopped obsessing over their deaths. I then just tried to remember ordinary memories, like conjuring up a picture in my mind of my mother's hands and face as she read the nightly newspaper at the kitchen table, or visualizing the joy on my father's face whenever he first laid eyes on my children when we came for a visit. These images started to replace the more painful ones, and I slowly began to feel some of the sadness leaving my body. The passage of time is surely helpful, but nothing will ever erase the deep love that I felt and feel for both of my parents, and the ache of wishing that they were still alive. It has been years since they both passed away, and I will never stop feeling fortunate to have grown up knowing that they were always by my side and that I could count on them for anything. I never doubted their love for me for a second! What a beautiful gift for parents to give to a child!

What I Learned:

I do not believe that anything can ever "prepare" you for the death of a loved one. As I have stated, my father's death was totally unexpected, and even though there were times that I hoped in some ways that my mother would be released from her body because she had been in pain for so long and was ready to go, I was certainly not prepared when she passed away. Both deaths brought me tremendous sorrow. For my own selfish reasons, I was clearly not ready for either of my parents to leave me. But it happened, and there was absolutely nothing that I or anyone else could do about it.

The grief process is different for everyone. When you lose your loved one, do whatever _you_ need to do to walk through the grief. Don't deny it and don't hurry it. Just go at your own pace, and your body and mind will let you know when you are ready to start emerging from your grief cocoon. Seek out support only if and when you need and want it. There were many times when I just needed and wanted to be left alone to think. Grief turned out to be very introspective for me, although it may not be that way for you. Your family and friends can literally and figuratively hold your hands and be by your side while you go through the grief process, but ultimately, you have to dig deep and find the strength within yourself to propel you forward and through it.

Away from Home

Holly

Metaphorically speaking, I was in a sea of sadness. I felt that I needed to be more grounded, to set anchors that would provide me with more stability and comfort. What really helped me? It was revisiting my childhood memories.

I often found comfort as I lay awake and imagined that I was at my childhood home, enjoying time with mom and dad and others who were no longer with me. I placed myself in situations that made me feel as if I were in a safe and happy place. I felt like I was on a ship and anchored in several ports.

My summers were spent at the beach in Canada, where we had a summer cottage. When I think about those days at the cottage, it brings back some of my very best memories. Almost daily, I would take long walks with my mom, my aunt and other friends to a local grocery store. Oftentimes, we would veer off onto different, but familiar paths while on our outings, and talk the time away. I'd often stop by myself at a local farm for fresh corn, and when I brought it back to our house, I would hear mom in the kitchen preparing food for friends and family who had stopped by to say hello. We always had many visitors, and the house was filled with love and laughter.

After my mom passed away, I sometimes imagined myself sleeping in my cottage bedroom with the night air breezing through my window, and being awakened by the tremendous thunderstorms that would rock our cottage. The crickets sang their song and an occasional skunk would emit a waft of foul scent that would inevitably rouse me from a deep sleep. These visualizations brought me great comfort and put a smile on my face. Of course, this happiness was shared with the sadness of knowing that those days were gone. I realize that for some people, it may be too painful to revisit whatever were your days of pure joy.

In addition to revisiting cherished memories, it is also human nature to relive our most painful memories. Over and over, I would go back to the bad days and ask myself how all this could have happened. No matter how I play it out in my mind, nothing changes. Although I was fortunate to be with my dad when he passed away, I was out-of-town when my mom suddenly took a turn for the worse. Even though I was with her the week before, the guilt of not being there when she passed away was initially monumental; now I choose to believe that it was G-d's plan for me not to be there. Either way, I will never know. What I do know is that she knew she was a wonderful mom, who was much loved, and that she is in our hearts forever.

During my grieving, there were times when I was suddenly overwhelmed by a heart-wrenching memory that seemed to come from out of the blue. Those kinds of flashes were totally out of my control. It does seem like we should be able to organize the good, the bad, and the neutral memories in different compartments and either retrieve them or keep them packed away.

Wouldn't it be great if we could just put all the hurtful times in a box and file it under "closed", while leaving only the good memories to savor? Unfortunately, no such luck! However, time is kind and will allow you to slowly let go of the bad memories and your "what if" thoughts. Time will also allow you to let go of the pain, bit by bit.

What I Learned:

Perhaps you have wonderful moments that you can revisit. Sometimes it takes time to remember them as it can be so painful. Don't be afraid to set your sail and anchor in different places of happiness. Our parents left a legacy to be remembered and cherished. Those memories are part of who I am today, and will help to sustain me for the rest of my life. They will also serve as a reminder as to how fortunate I am to have had such loving parents, who worked so hard to create a good life and special memories for my brother and me.

Crying In My Crackers

Holly

It was another night... sliding out of bed and marching to the kitchen searching for some type of relief. I was thinking of my friend's mom who had recently passed away. Then I focused on losing my own mom. These thoughts triggered my grief, and at 1:00 in the morning, I found myself wallowing in self-pity, only to seek comfort with a healthy helping of crackers and cheese. As the tears rolled down my cheeks, I found that I was literally crying in my crackers, while mindlessly eating away in an attempt to reign in my sadness.

I later discovered that another friend of mine was up at the exact same time as I was, also sobbing, because she was thinking about her mom, who had passed away within the last year. What is the probability of that? I learned this information when we spoke the following day. She confided that part of her never thought that she would be able to feel happy again because her mom was gone. On the flip side, when she actually did feel happy, she felt that she was betraying her mother. When a third friend's mom also recently passed away, she told me how surreal the whole experience had seemed to her. Since we are the baby boomers, I guess that it is pretty common for similarly aged friends to lose their parents these days.

The reason that I mention these friends of mine is that it reminded me that I was not alone, just as you are not alone. There are so many of us, men and women, who go through a similar process, yet find few people to help us along the way. When you can openly discuss and share your feelings with people you trust, or people going through a similar journey, the result is that you feel supported, some of the tension that you are carrying around gets released, and you recognize that other people can truly empathize with you in this most stressful phase of life.

I know that it was always helpful to me when Lauren and I shared our feelings about our moms. It created an even stronger bond between us and ended up being a healthy way for me to start the path to healing.

What I Learned:

Some of the reasons for writing this book are to let you know that you are not going crazy, you are not fixating, and you are not just depressed...you are mourning and yet celebrating the life of one of the most important and dearest people in your life. Please know that it's ok to be a little crazy or to "cry in your crackers" or whatever else it takes to bring you some relief from the heartache. Peaceful memories will evolve...it just takes time, and the grief timeline is different for everyone.

Will We Meet Again?

Holly

My hope is that when I die, I will make my way to heaven and be greeted by my parents, family and friends as they were prior to their illnesses...when they were happy, whole, talking and laughing. I wonder what they would say to me. I hope that they have been watching over me throughout the years.

Will we meet again? I believe we will.

Have you ever thought that you saw someone who resembled a loved one that had passed away? I know that I have. There have been a few women that I've seen who looked so much like mom that I had to resist the urge to run to them and give them a hug. My husband and I frequent an Italian restaurant in our neighborhood. On a recent visit, I immediately noticed someone who strongly resembled my mom. I later learned that this woman was the owner of the restaurant. Upon reflection, I think that maybe my mom "arranged" for us to go to this restaurant on this particular night, and "arranged" for the owner to be there at the same time so that I would see her when I walked in, and perhaps this would bring me some comfort.

Will we meet again? I believe we will.

Have you ever looked at the stars and had a feeling that your loved ones were once again with you at a given moment? Have you ever felt the strong presence of someone in the room whom you were very close to prior to his or her death? You know what I mean...that momentary shiver, and then your intuition kicks in and you are certain that you are no longer alone. This feeling has only happened to me a few times. Some people are lucky enough to dream about their parents and see them as if they were really there. I used to close my eyes and pray that I could see my parents in my dreams. But they have never appeared. If only I could see them and talk with them one more time.

What I would give for just a few moments...sometimes I close my eyes and feel their presence. I can hear their voices, see their faces, and feel their touch. To this day, I keep searching for ways to bring them back. Of course, they are always in my heart. Just the other day I brought out videos and watched wonderful family moments. Although it was painful at first, it ultimately made me happy to see mom and dad and hear their voices again, if only on the screen. It turned out to be therapeutic to see them the way they were before dementia robbed them of so much.

For many people, I suspect that it might be too painful to relive memories that were once such happy ones.

Will I ever see them again? I believe I will. My hope is that they will have no recollection of all the pain and suffering that they had to endure in their final years on earth.

What I Learned:

For those of you who have lost loved ones and are subsequently able to have positive dreams about them, you are very fortunate. For those who believe in the afterlife, take comfort in the certainty that you will meet again.

If your loved one is still with you, I know that there will be times that he or she will try your patience or make you angry. However, don't let those negative feelings cheat you out of the many precious moments that you have left. You can never get them back.

How Do I Talk to Myself?

Holly

If my mom could communicate with me today, I believe that these would be the words that she would say:

You know I loved you from the day you were born
Loved everything about you even though you tried my patience
You were my little girl and always will be
I am watching out for you even though you cannot see me.

Never give another thought to what has happened to me
In life there were many things I could not control and neither could you
Words that I may have said because my mind was ill
Those words were biting but never meant to hurt.

You were my best friend and advocate
And I am so proud of my children
I know it was very difficult for you to see me in certain states
I could not control my mind but I could control my love for you.

I had a wonderful life because you were in it
I may not have wanted to go on with my dementia in place
But you were my champion, my daughter, my friend.

Because of you I had a great life

I thank you for being there for me with the good and the not so good
I thank you for being patient with me
And that you did all you could and even more.

Don't cry for me even though I know that you still do
I'm your angel in the sky
Just look up and smile
And one day when it's your time, you'll "Come Fly with Me".

Magic Wand

Holly

It's such a helpless feeling...I always wanted to fix it. I wanted to make my parents well again...
My grandniece, who was four years old at the time, made up a song which essentially says:

"I'm looking for my magic wand, my magic wand, my magic wand.
I need that magic wand so there won't be any sickness or dying.
I need my magic wand to make everyone well and happy.
I'm looking for my magic wand."

It hit me when she sang it with so much feeling and conviction. She was dancing and singing with such innocence. My mom would have been proud of such an insightful little girl. I wish she had known her and her brother at this age because they are her beautiful great grandchildren. Hopefully, she's watching over them and smiling, and holding **her** magic wand.

What I Learned:

For those who have a parent with dementia, you have a tendency to try to fix them. We want to make everything better or go back to the way it was. "If I say this to you, or hug you, or take you someplace, then maybe you'll go back to the way you were, at least for a moment." But that doesn't happen, and you cannot fix it. You can only fix your expectations and the guilt that you are experiencing. *Find that magic wand that allows you to forgive yourself and allows you to accept your loved one as they continue on their intended path.*

Letter to My Friends

Holly

Thank you for being there for me.
Your intense kindness and love
I needed to vent and
You heard me.
No advice but pure listening
To the outcries in times of crises...

There are no words
Just heartfelt gratitude
Saving me from myself
And giving me the strength
To help my mom and dad.

And you are my angels
No one could surpass
What you have done for me
My lifelong friends...

Whenever you need someone
To listen
Know that I will always...
Be here for you.

Maybe One Day

Holly

Maybe one day I'll see you...
Maybe one day I'll come by and visit...
Maybe one day I'll take you out and
Maybe one day I'll have a party for you.

Maybe one day we'll reminisce
Maybe one day I'll wash your clothes
Maybe one day I'll sit and feed you and
Maybe one day I'll sing with you.

Maybe one day I'll bring the kids
Maybe one day we'll go for a ride
Maybe one day I'll stay for a while and
Maybe one day I'll just sit and listen.

But maybe tomorrow never comes
And my maybes never happen
And it's too late because you're gone
And I wish my maybes had turned into yeses.

What I Learned:

It's perfectly normal to be fearful or not want to see your loved one in their present condition. You may want to remember them the way they were. If you can, turn your maybe into "I will." Don't put off visits and interactions as the day may come when you wish you had shared time with a loved one. Each day brings precious moments.

Those memories may never be made if you wait until tomorrow.

My Email Angel

Holly

At the nursing home, there was a woman whose mom lived across the hall from my mom. I didn't really know her well, although we did have occasional conversations with one another. Since our attention was primarily focused on our moms, I think it was understood that there was no time for us to focus on any lengthy discussions. I didn't realize how precious she was until we started communicating through emails. Her name is Pat and she is my email angel.

Once we exchanged email addresses, I discovered that Pat was someone whom I could talk to, and we could help each other via our email messages. We would open ourselves up emotionally and try to console each other. I soon discovered that Pat is a very special lady. We shared our views and acknowledged each other's pain. Pat and I recognized that if we could reach out to at least one or two people in the nursing home who did not seem to have any visitors, we could bring some joy into their lives. As a result, Pat visited some residents and I made some phone calls to others.

I can't remember exactly when the emails began, but I know Pat's mom was still living and my mom had just passed away. Pat was such a comfort to me. I could talk to her instead of always baring my soul to my closest friends and family. We were like a sounding board for each other.

There were other "angels" who were strangers that offered consolation while my mom was in the nursing home. While I was crying in the nursing home parking lot one day, a woman tapped on my window and said that she totally understood why I was crying and what I was going through as she had been there before. We went for coffee and talked about our loved ones. It's so important to be understood and validated. That's why Lauren and I want to tell you that you are not alone... we've been there.

Getting back to my email angel, I would like to share some excerpts of a few of the emails that Pat and I exchanged, with the hope that you will see the value of having an email angel.

Pat: "Thanks for the love, prayers and email. I am doing ok. For years I have heard the expression "with a heavy heart" and now I know what it means. I am sure you feel it too. Not really something that you can explain but a definite weight of some sort in your heart... there is no preparation... I suddenly realized that the one and only person who loved me from the moment I was born was gone. You kept telling me to treasure the moments that I had with her and I did. I have wonderful memories and I am sure you do too. It makes it easier but it is so sad. Keep in touch".

Holly: "Your email was so beautiful. You're so right but I never thought about the expression "with a heavy heart" and it definitely describes what we're going through. And when you said that you suddenly realized that the one and only person who loved you from the moment you were born was gone brought tears (and happy tears) too, because they did love us from the day we were born and we loved them and still do... How lucky we were to have them for such a long time and to be blessed with such wonderful moms... Just wanted you to know that your emails touch my heart".

Pat: "...Holly, you will never know what your words and kindness mean to me. My life is a better place with you always there to help me out".

Holly: "...You are like my personal angel too. You can go on and on as much as you like. I love to listen and I'm here always. My mom was like that too".

What I Learned:

There are many opportunities for you to extend your hand and help others who are going through what you are or were experiencing. Even if you are a private person who does not want to talk about your situation with others, the day may come when you just need to vent. In that instance, all you need to do is look around you; you may be surprised to know that there are "angels" in your midst who want to surround you with love and understanding.

Section Six

Aftermath

Healing

Holly

Not a day goes by when I don't think of my mom, and it's been almost five years since she passed away. The hole in your heart starts once you recognize that you are dealing with an illness that you cannot control. The hole gets bigger with the hurt that you feel to see a loved one in such a compromised state. It really opened up wide for me when my mother left us. I experienced such an intense pain in the pit of my soul knowing that my mom, my best friend, my lifeline, would not be with me anymore. It's so hard to explain to someone who did not have a close relationship with a parent or who has not experienced losing a parent to dementia.

But I'm here to say that the hole narrows as time goes by. It's always there, but it gets filled with cherished memories, love, and familiar sounds and sensations. You can choose to fill it with grief and sorrow, but I don't think mom would have wanted that for my life. In fact, I know that she would have wanted me to be happy, and to hold dear all that she gave me throughout her life. Someone said to me recently that my voice and my intonations sounded just like my mom. What a fantastic compliment!

There is a time to heal...I feel I'm on the way and with each day I'm getting better. That is not to say you won't fall back to feeling sorrowful and sad. The extreme pain diminishes, and the sadness gets lighter. There is truth that the grieving process takes time, and that with time you will see positive change.

What I Learned:

Healing does not happen overnight. Be patient with yourself and others. Listen to your heart and listen to those you love. They may not always know what to say to you, and if they say something awkward, accept that they are still well meaning. When someone tells you that it is time to put the past behind you, ignore the comment and move on at your own pace.

You are the only one who can make that determination. Above all, remember to accept and to love yourself. You're on the path to healing...you are, after all, your parents' child, and they gave you some very special gifts that will help you with all of life's challenges.

Keep An Open Mind

Holly

We are confident that you can learn from us by reading this book. Please use our experiences to help guide you as you travel through this difficult and painful time with your loved one. Our thoughts and ideas can support you in coping with an aging parent or relative.

Please remember that you are the facilitator, the advocate. There will be nurses, doctors and other professionals who will want to give you advice. Sometimes it will be advice that you may feel is not always in the best interest of your loved one. Don't be afraid to challenge that advice and to do what you think is right with heartfelt conviction. If you were as fortunate as Lauren and I were to have wonderful parents who were always there for you, then no matter how difficult, accept the responsibility to care for them with as much love as they gave to you. Even if your parents were not the best parents, stand up, be the better person, and step into the caregiver role. You will never regret it because it is the right thing to do.

Be open to new techniques, innovations and ideas that may make life better for your loved one. Sometimes rules are rigid and unyielding in nursing homes, and protocol must be followed. However, that does not mean that the old ways are the right or the best ways. Go to the Director of the nursing home and suggest any ideas that you might have that would result in a positive difference. Change seldom happens without someone driving the bus, and that someone could be you!

Advocate, and if you don't know how to advocate, talk to someone who does know how (it is a skill), or seek help from a geriatric professional who has knowledge and experience, and can be part of your team.

What I Learned:

Find some common ground where you can work together with the professionals in a peaceful way. Sometimes opinions clash, and this could get in the way of helping your loved one. Don't be afraid to ask questions and to challenge techniques, but try to do it in a non-confrontational way if possible. (Sometimes it's not!) Everyone has an agenda that they are willing to defend. Our agenda is to create "home-like" nursing homes, staffed by knowledgeable professionals, where the emphasis is on a caring, supportive environment that always meets the best interests of its residents.

Promising Program

Lauren

While reading the August 21, 2016 Sunday edition of *The New York Times*, I came across an article in the Sunday Business section entitled "Private Equity's Stake in Keeping the Elderly at Home" by Sarah Varney. This article, which really grabbed my attention, focused on a little known 1990 Medicare program entitled "Program of All-Inclusive Care for the Elderly", or "PACE". (All of the following information about PACE is taken from this New York Times piece). PACE was designed to help older and disabled Americans live longer and more safely in their own homes, with the goal of preventing these at-risk individuals from requiring placement into a nursing home facility, thereby substantially reducing Medicare and Medicaid costs.

Under the PACE program, the senior in need enrolls at a PACE center, where there are medical offices, rehab facilities and food services, to list a few of the benefits, all run by a staff of medical professionals, social workers, physical therapists, etc. In exchange for a flat fixed monthly fee paid to PACE on behalf of the member by Medicare and Medicaid, PACE assumes ALL financial responsibility for the member by providing them with comprehensive and all-inclusive services (including covering the costs of hospitalizations). This comprehensive care even extends to the member's daily needs with services such as meals, transportation to and from the center, housekeeping, home health care, etc., if needed. Despite this overall assistance, participation in the PACE program is less costly than nursing home care, and hence, the savings to Medicare and Medicaid. (Note that all states require PACE costs to be kept below the cost of nursing home care).

Until recently, the government only allowed PACE to be run by non-profits. Several years ago, the government implemented a change which now allows PACE programs to be run by for-profit businesses as well. As a result of this change, there are a host of venture capitalists and entrepreneurs who have entered the PACE "market". Additionally, there are companies in the wings, including businesses within the tech industry, who are researching the possibilities of joining the ranks of PACE center operators, surely swayed by the reality of the upcoming substantial increase in the senior population as more baby boomers turn 60. (They undoubtedly recognize that this upswing in the senior market will also result in the need for more PACE centers).

I wish that I had known about PACE as my mother's illness became more debilitating. It is my opinion that she would have been a very good candidate for enrollment at a PACE center. My mom was a "joiner" and tried not to allow her very real aches and pains to take control of her life. She would have enjoyed and benefitted from what appears to be the strong socialization aspects of the program, and she would have relished the ease of having all her doctors in one place, vs. the hassle of traveling miles in any given week to her various appointments. However, as noted above, the PACE program was, and still is not well known. As of January 2016, there were only 40,000 people in the United States taking advantage of PACE services.

According to Ms. Varney, the article's author, there are professionals in related fields who worry about the effect of for-profits running PACE programs. They have concerns about commercialism diluting care levels, and worry about the centers being run with a business mentality vs. the social work mentalities of non-profits. In other words, PACE for profit centers has its critics.

As for my opinion, I must put you all on notice that I am not an expert on PACE. I know nothing about the program except for what I have read in Ms. Varney's article. However, I do know that I like, or even love PACE for one simple reason, which has absolutely nothing to do with who runs its centers. I love PACE, along with its recent transformation to include for-profit center operators, simply because it has sparked discussion among the important decision-makers, who have come to recognize that there can be better, less expensive alternatives to nursing home care. It would have meant the world to my mother and my whole family if my mother could have spent her later years as a member in a PACE center. It would have meant that she could have spent her days in a warm, vibrant, social setting that successfully met all her needs, while returning at the end of the day to live safely in her own home with the appropriate supportive services.

My only hope is that programs utilizing PACE-like concepts will not only proliferate, but will one day put an end to the sterile, "one size fits all" nursing home environments often seen today.

Options for a Better Future

Holly

According to an AARP report, 87% of older adults would like to remain in their own homes and age in place. By the year 2030, the number of people in our country over age 65 is expected to reach 71 million. By 2050, one-fifth of the total U.S. population, about 88 million people, will be age 65 and older. Based upon these projections, the U.S. is facing a monumental increase in its senior population. Therefore, it seems apparent that appropriate measures must be taken NOW to ensure that all seniors have the opportunity to live safely and happily in an affordable, sustainable, medically monitored living situation.

Other countries have dealt with their aging populations by taking unique approaches in making life more comfortable for seniors. For example, in 2009, the small village of Hogewey in the Netherlands, built with sponsor funding, was opened. Hogewey is essentially a community for dementia patients that allows residents to roam about freely, live in their own apartments without locks, and go about their daily life with few limitations. Residents can go grocery shopping, cross streets, enjoy each other's company and not feel constrained.

Another concept in the Netherlands offers free rent to students in living residences populated by seniors. In lieu of paying rent, students become companions/friends to senior residents who would otherwise live lonely and isolated lives. The students and seniors participate in activities together, such as watching sports and celebrating holidays. According to the International Association of Home and Service for the Aging, similar programs exist in France and Spain.

In the United States, grass-roots movements to help seniors are being developed at the community level. For example, a neighborhood village movement was started in Beacon Hill, Massachusetts, whereby neighbors watch out for each other, by helping those who need help with everyday tasks such as driving, cooking and running errands. This allows seniors in the community the ability to remain in their own homes, surrounded by a group of people with whom they can socialize and depend upon for assistance.

When discussing alternatives to conventional nursing homes, we would be remiss in not mentioning "The Eden Alternative." This is a philosophy created by Dr. William Thomas, a nursing home doctor, who, along with some of his staff, recognized the massive problems inherent in all traditional nursing home settings. The Eden Alternative principles can be used by nursing home staff and family members to transform the impersonal institution nursing home model to one that promotes a culture that is people-centered, and populated with gardens, animals, and ongoing activities. Everything is designed to stimulate the mind, while giving seniors more control over all aspects of their own care. (This philosophy is outlined in Dr. William Thomas' book, *Life Worth Living*.)

As noted above, this small sampling of existing programs gives you an idea as to what can be done for our seniors, sometimes in lieu of living in a nursing home. Fortunately, there now appears to be a positive attitudinal shift toward finding the right solutions for our aging population so as to enable them to live out their lives in happiness and dignity.

Regrettably, none of these outlined programs were available for our moms. At the time that our mothers became ill, Lauren and I were both faced with the fact that a nursing home was the only viable placement that would ensure their safety and wellbeing, given our respective financial constraints. If we could have kept our mothers in their own homes, we would have been faced with the astronomical and impossible to meet costs of 24/7 in-home care. Even if both of our mothers had had long-term health care insurance, which neither did, it would not have covered all the costs of the care that they both needed.

In the foreseeable future, there will undoubtedly be many seniors who will need care in one form or another, but will not be able to afford the costs. Medicaid, Medicare and state and local governments will be unable to keep up with the costs of a burgeoning senior population. Changes must be made NOW. The old system of caring for our elderly is broken, and new, less costly, but more innovative solutions are already in existence. Medicare and Medicaid need to wake up and funnel monies into these alternative programs that allow seniors to age in place instead of continuing to support outdated nursing home facilities. We also hope that that there will be additional private and/or public funding that would serve to mitigate the costs of aging in place. We crowdfund ideas, we raise monies for certain causes.... we must now do whatever we need to do need to supplement those who have no other option than going to a skilled nursing facility, by trying to help them and keep them safe in their own homes.

Regrets

Lauren

Yes, I do have some personal regrets, but if I were to go back in time, what could I have changed? I could not have changed the course of my mother's illness. My brother is a doctor and he was always on top of her medical issues, but he is not a wizard, and could not stop the progression of either her medical issues or her dementia. Although I do think that some of her doctors were not skilled in working with a geriatric patient, and while I questioned and still question their use of so much medication, I recognize that doctors are only human. Perhaps their willingness to try different medications, in different strengths and combinations to see if anything would work, was their reaction to my chronic requests for them to "make it better."

Although I am sure that I made quite a few mistakes on how I handled things throughout the many years of my mother's illness, I know that there was never a time when I gave up trying to help her and make things better for her. I am satisfied in knowing that I was always dedicated to her care and comfort.

The things that I do regret are things that were really out of my control. I wish that nursing homes were not institutions, and were in fact, much more "home-like" than they really are. Unfortunately, there is very little about any of the nursing home that I have ever been in that reflects the comforts of being at home! I wish that nursing home aides were better paid, and therefore, the job would attract better trained and more qualified personnel. I wish that the staff of nursing homes were more "invested" in the nursing home, in that I mean I wish that nursing homes were structured so that employees could obtain a small ownership interest in the nursing home by performing their work successfully over a period of time. I believe that this type of an employment incentive would provide an external motivation for staff to continue to perform well. If residents are happy and well cared for, the facility attracts more clientele, ultimately making the facility more successful, thereby benefitting staff/owners.

I regret that for the most part, Western or American society does not honor the elders in our communities, but rather, the elderly are viewed as second-class citizens, meant to be seen, but not heard. When I am with a client in the presence of a third person, such as a nurse or a doctor, I cannot tell you how many times that third person will direct inquiries about the client to me, as if the client were not with us in the room. Do they think that when someone is elderly, they can no longer talk or comprehend?

I regret that most people do not take more of an interest in the elderly and spend time volunteering in elder care facilities or senior centers. I regret that many seniors, especially those without family, live out their final days lonely and afraid, sometimes in real fear that their money will run out before they die. There is something very wrong with a society and a government that rarely seems to be looking out for the best interests of seniors. How did things get this way and what can we do about it? I believe that by putting our heads together, we can come up with a plan of action.

What I Learned:

Throughout the course of writing this book, both Holly and I came to the conclusion that we needed to develop a viable plan of action to institute some very real and substantial changes within the nursing home industry by making legislative changes at the state and/ or federal level. We need your help to do this, and would appreciate it if you could email us with your concerns and recommendations about improving nursing home care to:

lovelossdementia@gmail.com. We would also like to hear from you regarding your personal stories about having a loved one with dementia at home, or living in a nursing home. We promise to personally review each and every email that we receive, and work to integrate your stories, along with your suggestions, into a plan for transformation (and perhaps a follow-up book). In numbers there is strength; let's see what can be accomplished if we all join together to make CHANGE happen!

Acknowledgements

A great deal of time and effort has gone into the writing of this book. First and foremost, we must thank our families.

Holly:
To my husband Henry, who was by my side every step of the way and supported me by providing invaluable feedback and hugs when needed.

To my brother Alan, thank you for consistently being there for me, as well as for mom and dad. I am so thankful for a brother like you.

To my son David, who supported me along the way and challenged me to give my best.

Lauren:
To my husband Dana, and to my daughter Jessica, thank you for your continued support and for allowing me uninterrupted time to devote to this labor of love.

To my son Daniel, thank you for your review of our work and for your spot-on critiques; you always steered us in the right direction.

To my brother Elliott, thank you for your immeasurable help on this book, for always having my back, and for being such a supportive partner as we traveled down this uncharted road together.

Holly and Lauren:

To our respective parents for providing us with unconditional love, and the foundation to believe that we could accomplish anything. We are so grateful that you were our parents, and love and miss you always.

To our many early readers, thank you for assuring us that what we had to say was valuable, in that it could provide comfort and assistance to other people who were going through the same or similar experiences.

To all our family and friends too numerous to mention, we could not have written this book without your love and encouragement.

Cover design created using Freepik.

94301981R00093

Made in the USA
Columbia, SC
25 April 2018